The Complete Vocal Score of Handel's Messiah
Plus Forty Traditional Carols of Christmas

Amsco Publications
New York/London/Paris/Sydney/Copenhagen/Berlin/Tokyo/Madrid

Editor: Amy Appleby
Editorial Assistant: Elaine Adam
Music restoration and engraving: Anne Denvir

Order No. AM 980683
US International Standard Book Number: 0.8256.2965.9
UK International Standard Book Number: 1.844449.633.3

Exclusive Distributors:
Music Sales Corporation
257 Park Avenue South, New York, NY 10010 USA
Music Sales Limited
8/9 Frith Street, London W1D 3JB England
Music Sales Pty. Limited
120 Rothschild Street, Rosebery, Sydney, NSW 2018, Australia

Printed in the United States of America by
Vicks Lithograph and Printing Corporation

CONTENTS

Messiah

PART I

PART II

Messiah

PART II (CONT'D)

PART III

Carols of Christmas

G.F. HANDEL

MESSIAH

AN ORATORIO

Edited by
T. TERTIUS NOBLE

Revised according to Handel's original score
by
MAX SPICKER

VOCAL SCORE

allegro
pian
pian
Glory to God
in the Highest
and
and Peace on Earth

INTRODUCTORY NOTE

MESSIAH, Handel's most successful and best-known oratorio, was composed in the year 1741 in twenty-four days, from August 22 to September 14. It was first performed at a concert given for charitable purposes at Dublin, Ireland, on April 13, 1742, Handel conducting the performance in person.

According to the historical evidence, Handel knew that the Dublin orchestral and choral resources were by no means on a par with those of London and was markedly influenced by this circumstance in the composition of his work. In his choruses he did not go beyond four-part writing, and kept his orchestra within the most modest limits, so that no instrument except violin and trumpet plays a solo part, and oboe and bassoon do not appear at all in the score, although these instruments participated in the performance, as was proved by a later discovery of orchestra-parts written for both. Thereafter Handel, beginning with March 23rd, 1743, brought out the *Messiah* every year in London with great applause; in the course of time he made various alterations in certain numbers, set several new ones to music, transcribed a few arias for different voices, but left the work as a whole unchanged, both vocally and instrumentally, from its original form; thus bearing witness that, despite its limitations, this primitive conception of the work was likewise the enduring one.

As the centuries have passed, a considerable number of vocal scores have, of course, been made after Handel's partition; notably by Dr. Clarke (Whitfield-Clarke, 1809), and a later one by Vincent Novello. Their value, however, was more or less doubtful, their character being rather that of transcriptions in pianoforte style, with not infrequent arbitrary or capricious aberrations, than a faithful and exact reduction of the orchestral score. Neither have the more recent editions of vocal scores based on the Mozart orchestra-score, with its many contrapuntal charms, quite fulfilled expectations, as they materially increased the difficulty of the piano part.

Hence, a vocal score which should be in every way reliable and practical has become a matter of prime necessity. The present edition agrees at every point with Handel's original score, as it follows the facsimile edition of this latter with most careful exactitude. Slight deviations from the original, which in the course of many years have obtained almost traditional authority are inserted in small notes in every case, the professional artist being left free to employ them or not, at his discretion.

With regard to the performance of this grand work by chorus and soloists, much of importance might be said; but this would lead too far afield, and we shall, therefore, confine ourselves to the matters of chiefest concern. The direction of the choruses, which in our Master's works are for the most part peculiarly prominent in their monumental character, will naturally be entrusted to competent chorus-conductors, who will care for crystalline precision of execution and a clear logical conception, and who are responsible for these points.

The interpretation of their parts by the soloists in a different affair. Here we confront the weighty question: "May the soloist proceed subjectively, or must he proceed objectively?" Probably the best answer to this crucial query is found in a passage from the unrivalled work of an authority in this province, namely, "Die Lehre von der vokalen Ornamentik des 17. und 18. Jahrhunderts," by Dr. Hugo Goldschmidt. He writes: "The essence of reproduction, to feel and re-create that which was felt and imparted by the creator, does not exclude—within natural limitations—the assertion of creative power. The modern theory of æsthetics founded by Lipps rightly proceeds from the idea, that the interpreting artist creates, in a sense, the work anew. With his gradual penetration of the artwork he creates new values, which are of the highest importance for art, because without them, the creations of the great masters are only so much writing, and thus remain sealed to enjoyment. But the interpreter's work is no mere execution, comparable, let us say, to that of the builder who transmutes the architect's plans into material reality. His task is rather to seize the vital conception of the artwork, to blend it with his own ego and the views of his period, and thus to imbue it with life and effectiveness. Whether singer or instrumentalist, he is a child of his time. His artistry is a product of its mental culture. It develops and changes with the evolution of artistic requirements. His formative and emotional powers are derived from the spirit of the epoch to which be belongs. Consequently, we shall always approach the art productions of earlier times through the medium of our own spiritual and emotional nature. It follows, that the domain which such artistic reproduction may open to us, although of great extent, and as broad in scope as the points of contact with modern sensibility can reach, will be dependent in any given period on a constantly shifting relation to the treasures of former ages. The genuine, great masterworks of the past retain their importance; they are immortal; but our relations to them are not constant, and change with the changing impressionability of the times. We hear the works of these past-masters of former centuries—of Palestrina, Gabrieli, Handel and Bach, yes, even of Mozart and Beethoven—with other ears than our forefathers, or even than our grandfathers. What we have experienced since their time, whatever we have wrested to our eternal gain, this it is which sounds in those works to our ears. Much that charmed former generations has no effect on ours; so much is part and parcel of the time which gave it birth, and decays with its passing. Only what is exalted over time and place remains as eternal gain; and here, again, another generation finds new treasures that earlier ones passed by unheeding. This is the unfailing criterion of true greatness, that its creations continually beget ever-new, ever-changing values, that they bring to each successive generation new revelations. Consider the history of Handel's art. The eighteenth century, in its latter half, admired it in the form of arrangements by contemporaries, those by Mozart and Hiller. Our present-day musical interpretation—on Dr. Chrysander's initiative—has gone back to the historically authenticated form, and disclosed to us the true Handel in his full grandeur. But it owes its success, not to a recognition that things must be so because Handel would have them so, but because they appeal more directly to our sense and feeling than do the arrangements of the eighteenth and nineteenth centuries."

Such are the pregnant and weighty pronouncements of an experienced man, deeply versed in musico-historical lore and research. They should be of the highest value to the serious artist.

Here a word shall be said touching the employment of the appoggiaturas in the recitatives and (in isolated cases) also in the arias. They are, of course, not given in this edition, or indicated only very infrequently.

The *appoggiatura,* in Handel's works, must be treated with the utmost caution and nicest discrimination. It should never be regarded as a mere ornament, but always fulfil some declamatory, melodic, or harmonic function. Do not lose sight of the fact that the appoggiatura lends greater elasticity and emphasis to the flow of melody and declamation, and also to the musical expression; at the same time, one cannot be too careful not to introduce it too often, for this would doubtless produce an unpleasing and inadmissible monotony instead of enhancing the effect.

According to historical evidence, Handel permitted his singers to employ appoggiaturas, and even melismata and cadences, in the arias of his oratorios; he invariably insisted, however, that they should not be mere embellishments serving simply for outward display of vocal effect, but calculated to promote the melodic flow and declamatory expression, and must, consequently, possess musical meaning and value. Mistakes in the use of these ornaments can be prevented only by a thorough knowledge of the development of vocal embellishments, a certain penetration into the spirit of Handel's oratorios, and a refined taste in matters pertaining to musical æsthetics.

The appoggiatura is unquestionably the most important and most frequently employed among the ornaments, and a few general observations concerning the principles involved can hardly fail to be welcome; more especially as they are accompanied by a number of practical illustrations.

An appoggiatura is in place where its introduction brings about a diatonic succession, and more particularly across the bar, in order to avoid the leap of a third; for example, in No. 5, page 26:

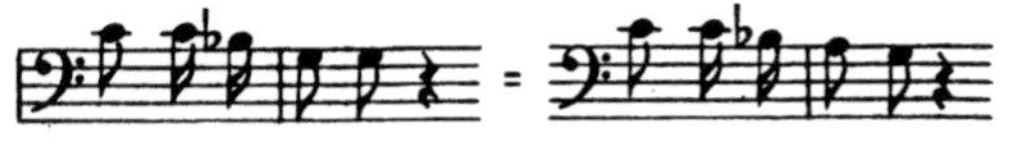

and similarly, within the boundaries of one measure, as in No. 19, page 94:

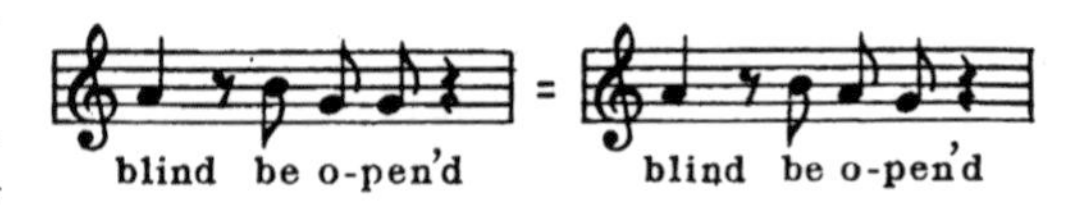

These latter must, however, be introduced with careful discrimination; otherwise appoggiaturas of this sort are very apt to produce a feeling of monotony and an interruption of the melodic flow. Another species of appoggiatura which may be used very effectively is the leap to the fourth below; this occurs both in the midst of a measure (No. 19, page 94)

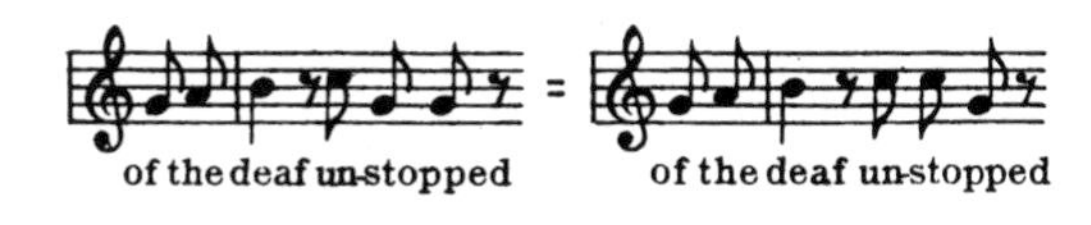

or (and far oftener) at the close of a recitative (No. 31, page 141):

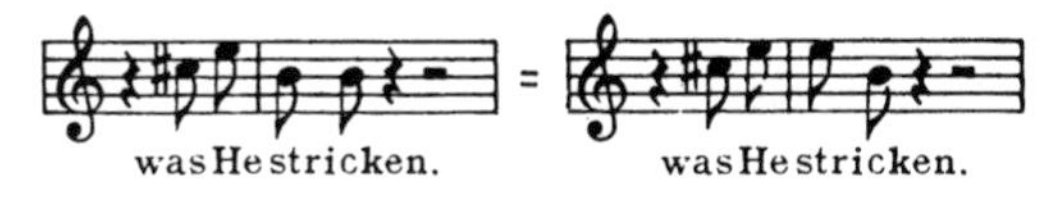

Besides these, the leap of the appoggiatura to the sixth below is occasionally met with (No. 2, page 9):

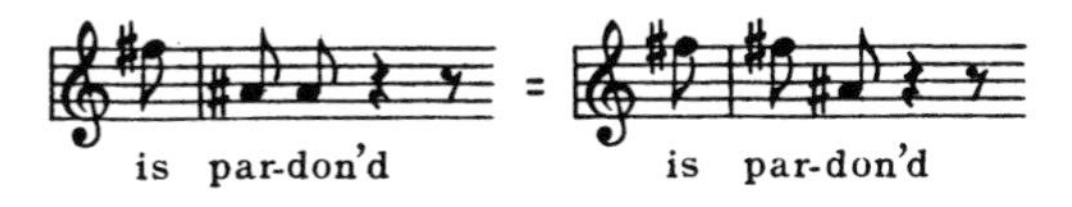

The appoggiatura leading upward by a step is seldom or never employed; leading up by a leap it is very successfully applied in certain cases, for example in No. 2, page 9:

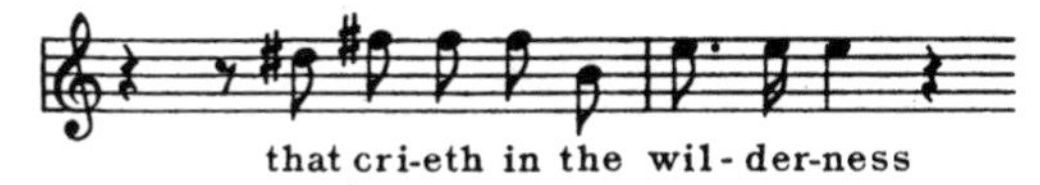

equivalent to

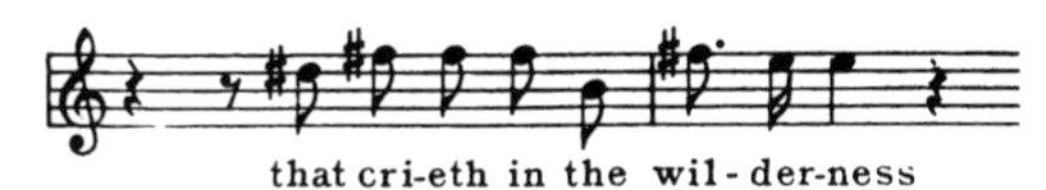

or No. 8, page 47:

Great discretion and sound judgment are, however, very necessary for governing the employment of this upward-leaping appoggiatura; for if, in a quite analogous situation, as shown in No. 5, page 25:

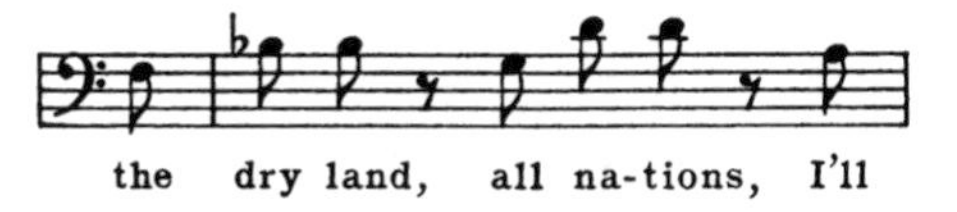

the appoggiatura were introduced at the similar points:

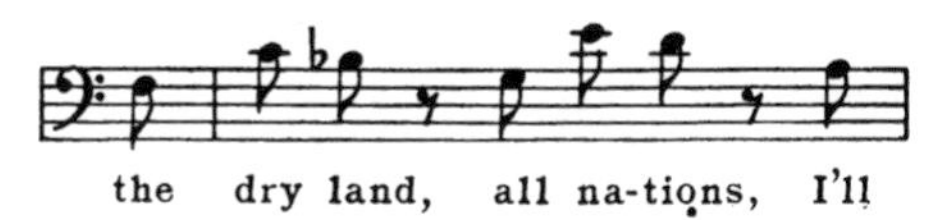

this would be, not simply a regrettable blunder, but a total misinterprettion of this important passage.

Illustrations of this kind show most convincingly how important it is that the singer should treat each case, as it arises, logically and discreetly, and how the appoggiatura, in apparently analogous situations, must sometimes be employed and at others avoided. The finest and most striking examples of this description, in our opinion, are those given by Handel in the *Messiah* on page 139 (No. 29): "Thy rebuke hath broken His heart," and on page 140 (No. 30): "Behold, and see." These two numbers, which are among the most beautiful, sublime, and affecting of all that Handel has given us in his oratorios, and which convey a sense of mournful, hopeless anxiety in a manner of almost unparalleled realism, should be attentively studied by every oratorio-singer who truly loves his art.

We seize this occasion to direct attention to another important matter, which ought to be mentioned, if for no other reason, because it is unnoticed in all the other vocal scores. We refer to the chorus "Glory to God!" page 82 (No. 17). Here Handel inserted in his original score the following phrase: *"da lontano e un poco piano"* (as from a distance, and rather softly); and only thus should this chorus be performed. It appears to us that, relying on Handel's directions for the dynamics of this number, there can be no doubt that he intended a gradual approach (augmentation) of this solemn chant, as of an increasingly urgent, divinely inspired announcement, followed by an equally gradual *decrescendo* withdrawal. Supporting evidence is found in the postlude, which, after a grand *fortissimo* climax of the chorus, dies away to a whispered *pianissimo.*

The authenticity of the above reading has occasionally been called in question, with argument both in speech and writing; but such questioning can rest only on a lack of acquaintance—or an inexact acquaintance—with Handel's original score. So, in order to settle this important point definitively, we publish at the beginning of this edition a facsimile of the first page of this chorus from Handel's original manuscript, which should suffice to set the question at rest forever.

In our edition the greatest care has also been bestowed upon the word-text, and each number provided with a correct reference to the corresponding section in the Bible.

We can, therefore, publish this edition with the consciousness that is has been prepared with the throughness and reverent care due to this eternally beautiful masterwork.

MAX SPICKER

TEXT

PART I

1. OVERTURE

2. RECIT. *Accompanied.* (TENOR)
Comfort ye, comfort ye my people, saith your God; speak ye comfortably to Jerusalem; and cry unto her, that her warfare is accomplishèd, that her iniquity is pardoned.

The voice of him that crieth in the wilderness, Prepare ye the way of the Lord, make straight in the desert a highway for our God.

3. AIR (TENOR)
Every valley shall be exalted, and every mountain and hill made low; the crooked straight, and the rough places plain.

4. CHORUS
And the glory of the Lord shall be revealèd, and all flesh shall see it together: for the mouth of the Lord hath spoken it.

5. RECIT. *Accompanied.* (BASS)
Thus saith the Lord of Hosts: Yet once a little while and I will shake the heavens, and the earth, the sea, and the dry land; and I will shake all nations, and the desire of all nations shall come.

The Lord, whom ye seek, shall suddenly come to his temple, even the messenger of the covenant, whom ye delight in; Behold, He shall come, saith the Lord of Hosts.

6. AIR (BASS)
But who may abide the day of His coming, and who shall stand when He appeareth?

For He is like a refiner's fire.

7. CHORUS
And He shall purify the sons of Levi, that they may offer unto the Lord an offering in righteousness.

8. RECIT. (ALTO)
Behold, a virgin shall conceive, and bear a Son, and shall call his name Emmanuel, God with us.

9. AIR (ALTO) AND CHORUS
O thou that tellest good tidings to Zion, get thee up into the high mountain; O thou that tellest good tidings to Jerusalem, lift up thy voice with strength; lift it up, be not afraid; say unto the cities of Judah, Behold your God!

Arise, shine, for thy light is come, and the glory of the Lord is risen upon thee.

10. RECIT. *Accompanied.* (BASS)
For, behold, darkness shall cover the earth, and gross darkness the people; but the Lord shall arise upon thee, and His glory shall be seen upon thee, and the Gentiles shall come to thy light, and kings to the brightness of thy rising.

11. AIR (BASS)
The people that walkèd in darkness have seen a great light: and they that dwell in the land of the shadow of death, upon them hath the light shinèd.

12. CHORUS
For unto us a Child is born, unto us a Son is given, and the government shall be upon His shoulder: and His name shall be called Wonderful, Counsellor, the Mighty God, the Everlasting Father, the Prince of Peace.

13. PASTORAL SYMPHONY

14. RECIT. (SOPRANO)
There were shepherds abiding in the field, keeping watch over their flocks by night.

RECIT. *Accompanied.* (SOPRANO)
And lo! the angel of the Lord came upon them, and the glory of the Lord shone round about them, and they were sore afraid.

15. RECIT. (SOPRANO)
And the angel said unto them, Fear not; for, behold, I bring you good tidings of great joy, which shall be to all people.

For unto you is born this day in the city of David a Saviour, which is Christ the Lord.

16. RECIT. *Accompanied.* (SOPRANO)
And suddenly there was with the angel a multitude of the heavenly host praising God, and saying:

17. CHORUS
Glory to God in the highest, and peace on earth, good will towards men.

18. AIR (SOPRANO)
Rejoice greatly, O daughter of Zion; Shout, O daughter of Jerusalem: behold, thy king cometh unto thee.

He is the righteous Saviour, and He shall speak unto the heathen.

19. RECIT. (ALTO)
Then shall the eyes of the blind be opened, and the ears of the deaf unstoppèd; then shall the lame man leap as an hart, and the tongue of the dumb shall sing.

20. AIR (ALTO)
He shall feed His flock like a shepherd; and He shall gather the lambs with His arm, and carry them in His bosom, and gently lead those that are with young.

AIR (SOPRANO)
Come unto Him, all ye that labour and are heavy laden, and He shall give you rest.

Take His yoke upon you, and learn of Him; for He is meek and lowly of heart, and ye shall find rest unto your souls.

21. CHORUS
His yoke is easy and His burthen is light.

PART II

22. CHORUS
Behold the Lamb of God, that taketh away the sins of the world.

23. AIR (ALTO)
He was despisèd and rejected of men: a man of sorrows and acquainted with grief.

*[He gave His back to the smiters, and His cheeks to them that plucked off the hair: He hid not His face from shame and spitting.]

24. CHORUS
Surely He hath borne our griefs, and carried our sorrows; He was wounded for our transgressions; He was bruisèd for our iniquities; the chastisement of our peace was upon Him.

25. CHORUS
And with His stripes we are healèd.

26. CHORUS
And we like sheep have gone astray; we have turnèd every one to his own way; and the Lord hath laid on Him the iniquity of us all.

27. RECIT. *Accompanied.* (TENOR)
All they that see Him, laugh Him to scorn, they shoot out their lips, and shake their heads, saying:

28. CHORUS
He trusted in God that He would deliver Him; let Him deliver Him, if He delight in Him.

29. RECIT. *Accompanied.* (TENOR)
Thy rebuke hath broken His heart; He is full of heaviness. He looked for some to have pity on Him, but there was no man; neither found He any to comfort Him.

30. AIR (TENOR)
Behold, and see if there be any sorrow like unto His sorrow.

31. RECIT. *Accompanied.* (TENOR)
He was cut off out of the land of the living: for the transgression of Thy people was He stricken.

32. AIR (TENOR)
But Thou didst not leave His soul in hell; nor didst Thou suffer Thy Holy One to see corruption.

33. CHORUS
Lift up your heads, O ye gates; and be ye lift up, ye everlasting doors; and the King of glory shall come in.

Who is the King of glory? The Lord strong and mighty, the Lord mighty in battle.

Lift up your heads, O ye gates; and be ye lift up, ye everlasting doors; and the King of glory shall come in.

Who is the King of glory? The Lord of Hosts, He is the King of glory.

34. RECIT. (TENOR)
Unto which of the angels said He at any time, Thou art my Son, this day have I begotten Thee?

35. CHORUS
Let all the angels of God worship Him.

36. AIR† (BASS)
[Thou art gone up on high, Thou hast led captivity captive, and receivèd gifts for men; yea, even for Thine enemies, that the Lord God might dwell among them.]

---

* *The latter part of this Air is usually omitted.*

† *This Air is usually omitted.*

37. CHORUS
The Lord gave the word: great was the company of the preachers.

38. AIR (SOPRANO)
How beautiful are the feet of them that preach the gospel of peace, and bring glad tidings of good things.

39. CHORUS
Their sound is gone out into all lands, and their words unto the ends of the world.

40. AIR (BASS)
Why do the nations so furiously rage together? [and] why do the people imagine a vain thing?

The kings of the earth rise up, and the rulers take counsel together against the Lord, and against His Anointed.

41. CHORUS
Let us break their bonds asunder, and cast away their yokes from us.

42. RECIT. (TENOR)
He that dwelleth in heaven shall laugh them to scorn; the Lord shall have them in derision.

43. AIR (TENOR)
Thou shalt break them with a rod of iron; Thou shalt dash them in pieces like a potter's vessel.

44. CHORUS
Hallelujah! for the Lord God omnipotent reigneth.

The kingdom of this world is become the kingdom of our Lord, and of His Christ; and He shall reign for ever and ever.
King of Kings, and Lord of Lords. Hallelujah!

PART III

45. AIR (SOPRANO)
I know that my Reedemer liveth, and that He shall stand at the latter day upon the earth:

And though worms destroy this body, yet in my flesh shall I see God.

For now is Christ risen from the dead, the first-fruits of them that sleep.

46. CHORUS
Since by man came death, by man came also the resurrection of the dead. For as in Adam all die, even so in Christ shall all be made alive.

47. RECIT. *Accompanied.* (BASS)
Behold, I tell you a mystery: We shall not all sleep; but we shall all be changed in a moment, in the twinkling of an eye, at the last trumpet.

48. AIR (BASS)
The trumpet shall sound, and the dead shall be raised incorruptible, and we shall be changed.

*[For this corruptible, must put on incorruption, and this mortal must put on immortality.]

49. RECIT.† (ALTO)
[*Then* shall be brought to pass the saying that is written: Death is swallowed up in victory.

50. DUET (ALTO AND TENOR)
O death, where is they sting? O grave, where is thy victory? The sting of death of sin, and the strength of sin is the law.

51. CHORUS
But thanks be to God, who giveth us the victory through our Lord Jesus Christ.

52. AIR (SOPRANO)
If God be for us, who can be against us? who shall lay any thing to the charge of God's elect? It is God that justifieth, who is he that condemneth?

It is Christ that died, yea, rather, that is risen again, who is at the right hand of God, who makes intercession for us.]

53. CHORUS
Worthy is the Lamb that was slain, and hath redeemed us to God by His blood, to receive power, and riches, and wisdom, and strength, and honour, and glory, and blessing.

Blessing and honour, glory and power, be unto Him that sitteth upon the throne, and unto the Lamb, for ever and ever.

Amen.

**The latter part of this Air is usually omitted.*

†This and the three following pieces are sometimes omitted.

THE MESSIAH

PART I

No. 1 – OVERTURE

G.F. Handel

Allegro moderato (♩= 116)
f
tr
L.H.
A
mf
B
f

C
mf
D
cresc.

E
f
F
ff
Più lento

No. 2 – RECITATIVE FOR TENOR

"Comfort ye my people"

Isaiah xl: 1-3

saith your God, saith your God;
fp
mf
speak ye com-fort-a-bly to Je-ru-sa-lem, speak ye
p simile
com-fort-a-bly to Je-ru-sa-lem, and cry un-to her that her
B 1)
mf
war - fare, her war - fare is ac-complished, that her in-
2)
p
Original orchestral score has:
1)
cry un-to her
2)
is ac-com-plish'd

i - qui - ty is par-don'd, that her in - i - qui - ty is par - -
don'd.
mf
C
The voice of him that crieth in the wilderness, Pre-pare ye the way of the
f
Lord, make straight in the desert a high-way for our God.

No. 3 – AIR FOR TENOR
"Every valley shall be exalted"

Isaiah xl: 4

ex-alt - - - - - - - - - - - - - - - -
- - - - - - - ed, shall be ex - alt - - ed,
shall be ex-alt - - - - - - - - - - - - - -
B
- ed, and ev-'ry moun - tain and hill made low;
f
p
p

the crook-ed straight, and the rough plac-es
plain,
the crook-ed
straight, the crook - ed straight, and rough plac-es plain,
cresc.
p
simile

— and the rough plac-es plain.
C
Ev-'ry val-ley, ev-'ry val-ley —
— shall be ex-alt - ed,
p
mf
f

D
ev-'ry val-ley,
ev-'ry val-ley shall be ex-alt-
-ed,
and ev-'ry moun-tain and
hill made low;
the crook-ed straight,
the
crook-ed straight, the crook-ed straight, and the rough plac-es plain,
f
p
tr

and the rough plac-es plain, and the rough plac-es
plain,
the crook-ed straight,
ad lib.
E
and the rough plac - es plain.
colla voce
senza Ped.
f a tempo
tr
p
f
cresc.

No. 4 – CHORUS
"And the glory of the Lord"

Isaiah xl: 5

*) According to the original score.

Lord shall be re -
Lord
Lord shall be re - veal - ed,
Lord shall be re - veal -
veal - ed, and the glo - ry, the glo-ry of the
shall be re - veal-ed,
and the glo - ry, the glo-ry of the Lord
- ed, shall be re - veal-ed,
A
Lord shall be re - veal'd, and the
be re - veal - ed, and the
shall be re - veal - ed, and the
and the
A

glo - ry, the glo-ry of the Lord shall be re - veal - ed,
glo - ry, the glo-ry of the Lord shall be re-veal - ed,
glo - ry, the glo-ry of the Lord shall be re-veal - ed,
glo - ry, the glo-ry of the Lord shall be re-veal - ed,
mf
and all flesh shall
see it to - geth-er,
mf
and all flesh shall see it to - geth-er;

B
and all flesh shall see it to - geth - - -
and all flesh shall see it to - geth -
for the mouth of the Lord hath spok-en
For the mouth of the Lord hath spok-en
B
er; for the mouth of the Lord hath spok - en
er, and all flesh shall see it to-geth - - -
it; and all flesh shall see it to-geth - - -
it; and all flesh shall see it to-geth - - -
it;
er, and all flesh, and all flesh shall see it to - geth-er;
er, and all flesh shall see it to - geth - - er; the
er, for the
C
C

and all flesh shall see it to - geth - - er;
and all flesh shall see it to - geth - er;
mouth of the Lord hath spok - en it.
mouth of the Lord hath spok - en it.
And the glo - ry, the glo-ry of the Lord, and all
And the glo - ry, the glo-ry of the Lord, and all flesh shall
And the glo - ry, the glo-ry of the Lord, and all flesh shall
And the glo - ry, the glo-ry of the Lord, and all
D
flesh shall see it to - geth - er; the mouth of the Lord hath
see it to - geth - er; and the glo - ry, the glo-ry of the
see it, shall see it to - geth - er;
flesh shall see it to - geth - er;
D

spok - en it,
Lord shall be re - - veal - ed, and all
and all flesh —
and all flesh —
for the mouth of the Lord hath
flesh — shall see it to - geth - er; for the
shall see it to - geth - er; the glo - ry, the glo - ry of the
shall see it to - geth - er;
E
spok - en it, hath — spok - - - - en it;
mouth of the Lord hath spok - en it; and all
Lord shall be re - veal - - - - - - - - ed,
and the glo - ry, the glo - ry of the Lord shall be re - veal - ed,
E

ff
and the glo - ry, the glo - ry, the
flesh_ shall see it to - geth - er;
and all flesh_ shall see it to - geth - er;
and all flesh shall see it to - geth - er;
glo-ry of the Lord shall be re - veal - - - ed,
ff
and the glo - ry, the glo-ry of the Lord shall be re -
ff
and the glo - ry, the glo-ry of the Lord
ff
and the glo - ry, the glo-ry of the Lord shall
and all flesh_ shall
veal - - - ed, re - veal-ed, and all flesh_ shall
shall be re - veal - - ed, and all flesh_ shall
be re - veal - - - ed, re - veal - - ed; for the mouth

F
see it to - geth - er, to - geth - - er; for the mouth of the
see it to - geth - er, to - geth - - er; for the mouth of the
see it to - geth - er, to - geth - - er; for the mouth of the
of the Lord hath spok - en it, for the mouth of the
F
Lord hath spok - en it, for the mouth of the
Lord hath spok - en it, for the mouth of the
Lord hath spok-en it, for the mouth of the Lord, the
Lord hath spok - en it, for the mouth of the Lord, the
Adagio
Lord hath spok - en it.
Lord hath spok - en it.
mouth of the Lord hath spok - en it.
mouth of the Lord hath spok - en it.
Adagio

No. 5 – RECITATIVE FOR BASS

"Thus saith the Lord"

Haggai ii: 6, 7 - Malachi iii: 1

*)Other editions have *C* here; according to the original score, however, *E* is correct.

of all na - tions shall come.
f
B
Recit.
The Lord whom ye seek shall suddenly come to His tem-ple, ev'n the
mes-sen-ger of the cov - e - nant, whom ye de - light in;
Be - hold, he shall come, saith the Lord of Hosts.

No. 6 – AIR FOR BASS

"But who may abide the day of His coming?"

Malachi iii: 2

B
He ap - pear-eth?
But who may a - bide, but
who may a - bide the day of His com-ing?
and
who shall stand when He ap - - pear - eth?
C
and who shall stand when
He ap - pear - - - - - - - - - -
mf
p
mp

eth? when He ap - pear -
D
eth?
Prestissimo (♩= 138)
pp
cresc.
f
For He is like a re -
p
fin - er's fire,
f

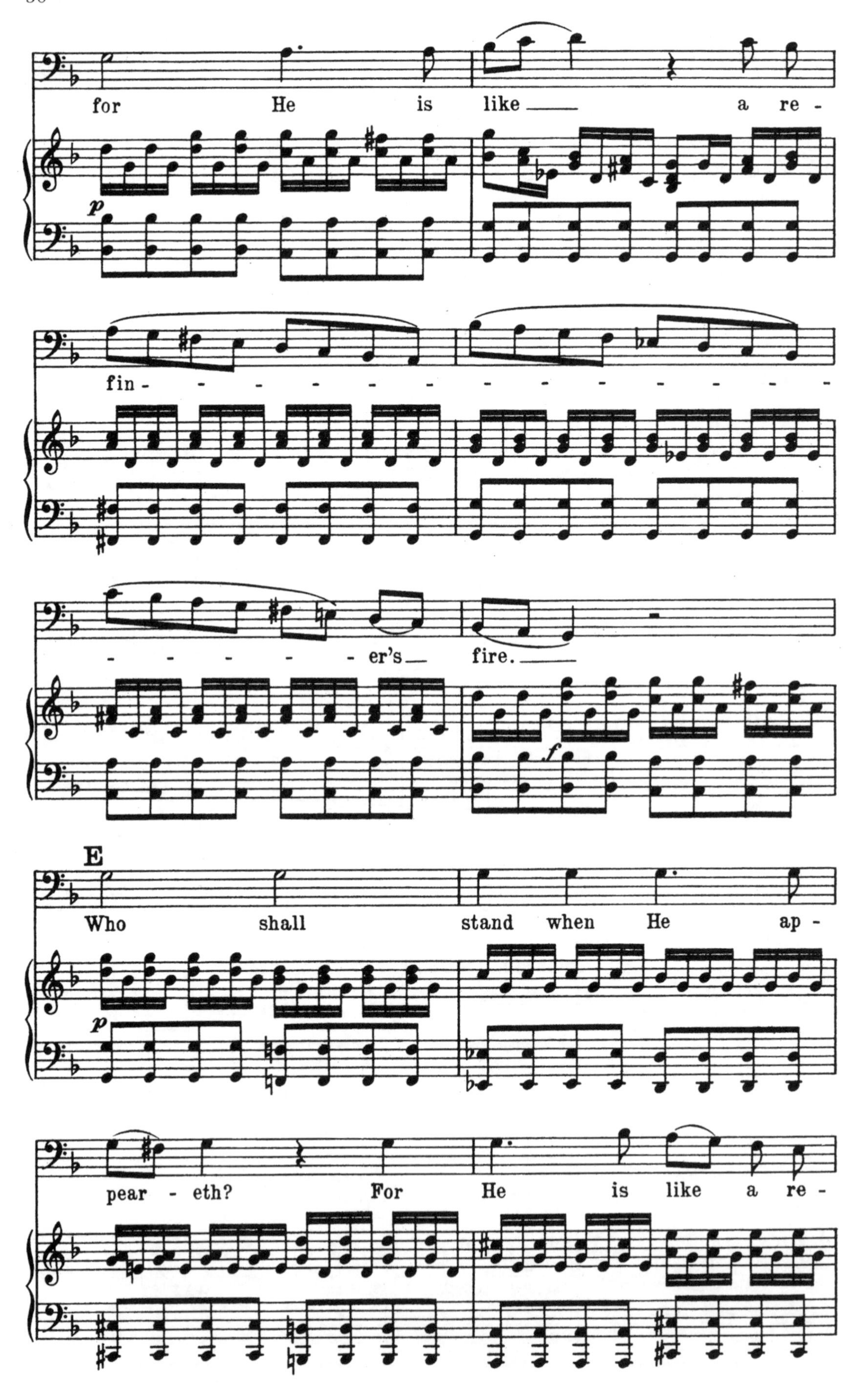
for He is like a re-
fin - - - - - - - - - - - - - - -
- - - - - er's fire.
E
Who shall stand when He appear - eth? For He is like a re-

fin - er's fire, for
He is like a re - fin - - - - - - - - - er's fire,
and who shall stand when He ap - pear-eth?
cresc.
colla voce

F Larghetto (Tempo I)
But who may a - bide the day of His coming?
p
mf
and who shall stand, and who shall stand when He ap -
p
peareth? when He ap - peareth?
f
G Prestissimo
For He is like a re - fin - - er's
p
f
p
fire, like a re - fin - - - er's
f
p

fire, and who shall stand when He,
when He ap - - pear-eth? and who shall
stand when He ap - - pear - eth?
H
For He is
like a re - fin - - - - - - er's
fp
p
cresc.

fire, and who shall
stand when He ap-
pear-eth, when He ap-
pear-eth? For He is
like a re-fin-
f
p
f
p
f
p
f
p
f
p

Adagio
- - - - er's fire, for He is like a re - fin - er's
cresc.
Prestissimo
fire.

No. 7 – CHORUS
"AND HE SHALL PURIFY"

Malachi iii: 3

pu - ri - fy, and He shall pu-ri-fy
A
mf
And He shall pu - ri - fy,
mf
And He shall pu-ri-fy
the sons of Le - - vi,
A
and He shall pu-ri-fy
the sons

and He shall pu - ri -
of Le - - - - vi,
and
fy
the sons of Le - - - -
and
He shall pu - ri - fy, and He shall pu - ri - fy the
the sons of Le - - - - - vi, the
vi, the sons
He shall pu - ri - fy
sons of Le - - - - - vi, the sons, the

B
sons of Le - vi, that they may of - fer
of Le - vi, that they may of - fer
the sons of Le - vi, that they may of - fer
sons of Le - vi, that they may of - fer
B
un - to the Lord an of - fer - ing in right - eous -
un - to the Lord an of - fer - ing in right - eous -
un - to the Lord an of - fer - ing in right - eous -
un - to the Lord an of - fer - ing in right - eous -
mf
ness, in right - eous - ness, and He shall pu - ri - fy,
f
ness, in right - eous - ness, and He shall
f
ness, in right - eous - ness, and He shall
f
ness, in right - eous - ness, and He shall
mf
f

mf
pu - - ri - fy,
pu - - ri - fy,
pu - - ri - fy, shall pu - ri - fy
mf
mf
f
and He shall pu - ri -
and He shall pu - - ri - - fy,
and He shall pu - - ri - - fy,
the sons of Le - - vi,
f

C
fy,
shall
and He shall
and He shall
and He shall
C
pu - ri - fy,
and He shall pu - ri - fy,
pu - ri - fy,
and He shall pu - ri - fy,
pu - - ri - fy,
and He shall pu - ri - fy,
pu - ri - fy,
and He shall pu - ri - fy, and

and He shall pu - ri - fy the sons, the sons of
He shall pu - ri - fy the sons of
He shall pu - ri - fy the sons of Le - vi, the sons of
Le - vi,
and He shall pu - ri - fy,
and He shall pu - ri - fy,
and He shall
Le - vi,
and He shall pu - ri - fy,
Le - vi,
and He shall pu - ri - fy,

D
pu - ri - fy the sons
and He shall pu - ri - fy
and He shall pu - ri - fy, shall pu - ri -
D
and He shall pu - ri - fy,
of Le - vi,
the sons of
fy the sons of Le - vi, the

shall pu - ri -
Le - - vi,
sons
of Le - - - -
and He shall pu - ri - fy
fy,
shall pu - ri - fy,
shall pu - ri - fy
the sons
vi,
and

the sons
shall pu - ri - fy the
of Le - - - - - - - - - -vi, the
He shall pu - ri - fy the sons, the
E
ff
of Le - vi, that they may of - - - fer
sons of Le - vi, that they may of - - - fer
sons of Le - vi, that they may of - - - fer
sons of Le - vi, that they may of - - - fer
E
ff

un - - to the Lord an of - fer - ing in right - eous - -
un - - to the Lord an of - fer - ing in right - - eous -
un - - to the Lord an of - fer - ing in right - - eous -
un - - to the Lord an of - fer - ing in right - - eous -
ness, in right - eous - ness.
ness, in right-eous - ness.
ness, in right-eous - ness.
ness, in right - eous - ness.
mf

No. 8 – RECITATIVE FOR ALTO

"Behold! a virgin shall conceive"

Isaiah vii: 14 - Matthew i: 23

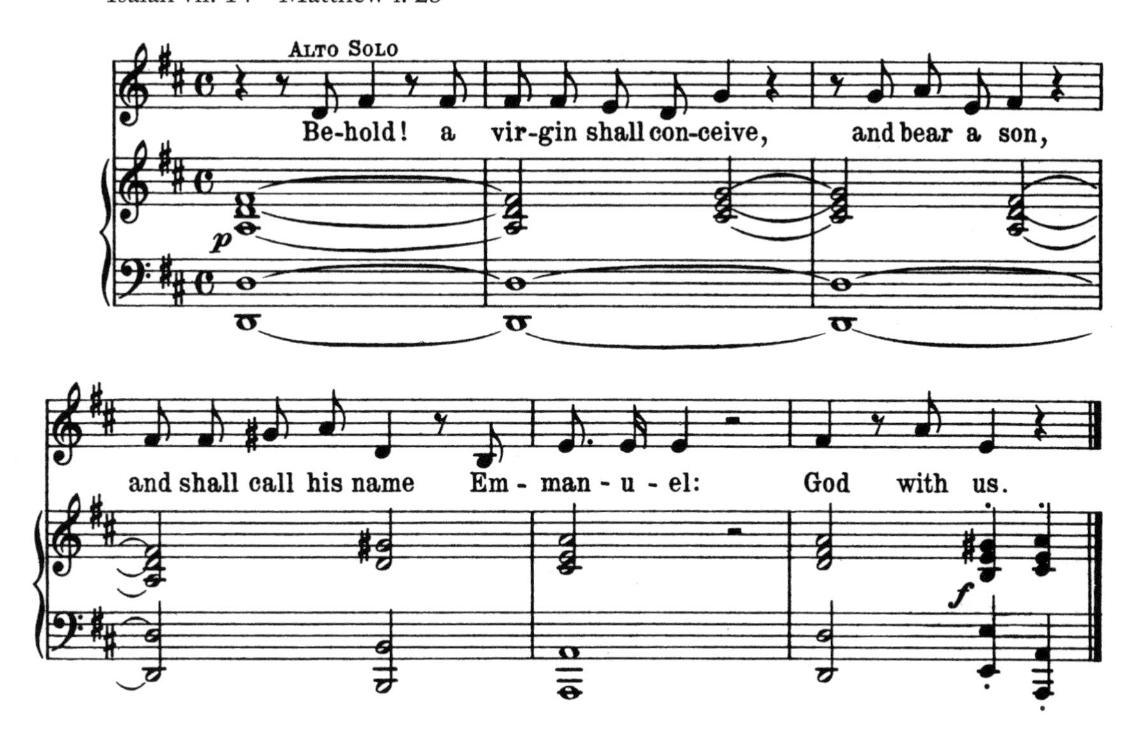

No. 9 – AIR FOR ALTO AND CHORUS

"O thou that tellest good tidings to Zion"

Isaiah xl: 9

Alto Solo
O
A
thou that tell-est good ti-dings to Zi-on,
get thee up in-to the high moun-tain!
O thou that tell-est good
B
ti-dings to Zi-on,
get thee

up in-to the high moun - - - - - - - - - - - -
- - - - - tain!
get thee up in-to the high
moun - - - - - - - - - - - - - - - - - - -
- - tain!
C
f
tr
tr
O
p

thou that tell-est good ti-dings to Je-ru-sa-lem, lift
mf
p
up thy voice with strength! lift it
D
up, be not a-fraid! Say un-to the
cit-ies of Ju-dah, say un-to the cit-ies of Ju-dah,
Be-hold your God! be-hold your God! Say

un-to the cit-ies of Ju - - - dah, Be -
hold your God! be - hold your God!
be - hold your God!
E
mf
O
p
thou that tell - est good ti-dings to Zi - on,
f

F
a - rise, shine, for thy light is come;
p
mf
a - rise, a -
p
rise, a - rise, shine, for thy light is come,
p
mf
and the glo - ry of the Lord, the
p
mf

G
glo - ry of the Lord is
ris - en, is ris - en up - on thee, is ris - en, is
ris - en up - on thee, the glo - ry, the
glo - ry, the glo - ry of the Lord
is ris - en up - on thee.
p
colla voce

CHORUS

53
O thou that tell - est good ti - dings to Zi - on, good
ALTO
TENOR
O
BASS
O thou that tell - est good
H
ti - dings to Je - ru - sa - lem, O
O thou that tell - est good
thou that tell - est good ti - dings to Zi - on,
ti - dings to Zi - on, good ti - dings to Je - ru - sa - lem,
thou that tell - est good ti - dings to Zi - on, good ti - dings to Zi - on, a -
ti - dings to Zi - on, to Zi - on, a -
O thou that tell - est good ti - dings to Zi - on, a -
a -

I
rise, a - rise, say un - to the cit - ies of
I
l.H.
Ju - dah, Be - hold your God! Be -
J
hold, the glo - - ry of the Lord is

ris - en up - - - - - - on thee. O
ris - en up - - - - - - on thee. O
ris - en up - - - - - - on thee. O
ris - en up - - - - - - on thee. O
K
thou that tell - est good ti - dings to Zi - on, say
thou that tell - est good ti - dings to Zi - on, say
thou that tell - est good ti - dings to Zi - on, say
thou that tell - est good ti - dings to Zi - on, say
K

un - to the cit - ies of Ju - - - - dah, Be -
un - to the cit - ies of Ju - - - - dah, Be -
un - to the cit - ies of Ju - - - - dah, Be -
un - to the cit - ies of Ju - - - - dah, Be -
f
hold, be - - hold,___ the
hold, be - - hold,___ the
hold, be - - hold, the
hold, be - - hold, the
mf

glo - ry of the Lord, of the Lord,
glo - ry of the Lord, of the Lord, the
glo - ry of the Lord, of the Lord,
glo - ry of the Lord, of the Lord,
the glo - - ry of the
glo - - ry of the Lord
the glo - - ry of the
the glo - - ry of the

Lord is ris - en up - on thee.
is ris - en up - on thee.
Lord is ris - en up - on thee.
Lord is ris - en up - on thee.
allargando
f
L
f

No. 10 – RECITATIVE FOR BASS

"For behold, darkness shall cover the earth"

Isaiah lx: 2, 3

A
but the Lord shall a - rise
poco cresc.
up - on thee, and His
glo - - - - - - ry shall be seen up - on thee, and His
glo - - - ry shall be seen up - on thee.
And the Gentiles shall
come to thy light, and kings to the brightness of thy ris - ing.
f

No. 11 – AIR FOR BASS

"The people that walked in darkness"

Isaiah ix: 2

walk-ed in darkness have seen a great light,
B
the peo-ple that walk-ed, that walk-ed in dark-ness, that
walk-ed in dark - ness, the peo-ple that walk-ed in dark - - -
- - - - ness have seen a great light, have seen a great light,
a great light, have seen a great light:
mf
p
mf

C
and
they that dwell, that dwell in the land of the shad - - - -
- ow of death,
and
they that dwell, that dwell in the land, that dwell in the land of the
shad-ow of death,
up -

D
on — them hath the light shin - - ed,
and
mf
p
they that dwell, — that dwell in the land of the shad - - - - -
- - ow of death,
up - on — them hath the
mf
p
light — shin - ed, up - on — them hath the light shin - ed.
mf

No. 12 – CHORUS

"For unto us a Child is born"

Isaiah ix: 6

us a Child is born:
un-to us a Son is giv-en, un-to
B
us a Son is giv-en:
For un-to us a Child is born,
For un-to
B
un-to us a Son is giv-en, un-to
us a Child is born,

us a Son is giv-en, un-to us a Son is
un-to us a Son is giv-en:
C
mf
and the gov-ern-ment shall
giv-en:
and the gov-ern-ment shall be up-on His shoul
C
mf
cresc.
be up-on His shoul - der, up-on His shoul-der; and His
mf
and the gov-ern-ment shall be up-on His shoul-der; and His
der;
and His
and the gov-ern-ment shall be up-on His shoul-der; and His
cresc.

D
Name shall be call-ed Won - der-ful, Coun - sel-lor,
Name shall be call-ed Won - der-ful, Coun - sel-lor,
Name shall be call-ed Won - der-ful, Coun - sel-lor,
Name shall be call-ed Won - der-ful, Coun - sel-lor,
D
The might-y God, The ev - er - last - ing Fa - ther, The Prince of Peace.
The might-y God, The ev - er - last - ing Fa - ther, The Prince of Peace. Un - to
The might-y God, The ev - er - last - ing Fa - ther, The Prince of Peace.
The might-y God, The ev - er - last - ing Fa - ther, The Prince of Peace.
us a Child is born, un - to us a Son is
For un - to us a Child is born,

p
Un-to us a Child is born,
giv-en:
mf
and the gov-ern-ment shall
p
un-to us a Son is giv-en:
be up-on His shoul
mf
and the gov-ern-ment shall be up-on His shoul
cresc.
and His Name shall be call-ed
E
ff
Won-der-ful,
der; and His Name shall be call-ed
Won-der-ful,
and His Name shall be call-ed
Won-der-ful,
der; and His Name shall be call-ed
Won-der-ful,
cresc.
ff

Coun - sel-lor,
The might - y God,
The
Coun - sel-lor,
The might - y God,
The
Coun - sel-lor,
The might - y God,
The
Coun - sel-lor,
The might - y God,
The
ev - er - last - ing Fa - ther, The Prince of Peace.
p
For un - to
ev - er - last - ing Fa - ther, The Prince of Peace.
ev - er - last - ing Fa - ther, The Prince of Peace. Un - to us a Child is born,
ev - er - last - ing Fa - ther, The Prince of Peace.
us a Child is born,
For un - to us a Child is born,
For un - to us a Child is born,
un - to

p
un-to us a Son is
p
un-to us a Son is
us a Son is giv-en:
giv-en:
mf
and the gov-ern-ment shall
mf
giv-en: and the gov-ern-ment shall be up-on His shoul - - - der;
mf
be up-on His shoul - - - der;
cresc.
and His
mf
cresc.
and the gov-ern-ment shall be up-on His shoul-der; and His
cresc.
and His
mf
cresc.
and the gov-ern-ment shall be up-on His shoul-der; and His
mf

F
Name shall be call - ed Won - - der - ful,
Name shall be call - ed Won - - der - ful,
Name shall be call - ed Won - - der - ful,
Name shall be call - ed Won - - der - ful,
F
Coun - - sel - lor, The might - y God, The
Coun - - sel - lor, The might - y God, The
Coun - - sel - lor, The might - y God, The
Coun - - sel - lor, The might - y God, The
ev - er - last - ing Fa - - ther, Prince of Peace. For un - to
ev - er - last - ing Fa - - ther, Prince of Peace. For un - to
ev - er - last - ing Fa - - ther, Prince of Peace. For un - to
ev - er - last - ing Fa - - ther, Prince of Peace. Un - to us a Child is born, un - to

us a Child is born,
us a Child is born,
us a Child is born, un - to us a Son is
us a Child is born, un - to us a Son is
giv - en, un - to us a Son is
giv - en, un - to us a Son is
un-to us a Son is giv-en: and the gov-ern-ment, the gov-ern-ment shall
un-to us a Son is giv-en: and the gov-ern-ment shall
giv-en, un-to us a Son is giv-en:
giv-en, un-to us a Son is giv-en:

be up-on His shoul - - - - der, and the gov-ern-ment shall
be up-on His shoul-der, and the gov-ern-ment shall
and the gov-ern-ment, the gov-ern-ment shall
and the gov-ern-ment, the gov-ern-ment shall
be up-on His shoul-der; and His Name shall be call-ed
be up-on His shoul-der; and His Name shall be call-ed
be up-on His shoul-der; and His Name shall be call-ed
be up-on His shoul-der; and His Name shall be call-ed
G
ff
Won-der-ful, Coun-sel-lor,
Won-der-ful, Coun-sel-lor,
Won-der-ful, Coun-sel-lor,
Won-der-ful, Coun-sel-lor,
G

The might-y God, The ev-er-last-ing Fa-ther, The Prince of Peace, The
The might-y God, The ev-er-last-ing Fa-ther, The Prince of Peace, The
The might-y God, The ev-er-last-ing Fa-ther, The Prince of Peace, The
The might-y God, The ev-er-last-ing Fa-ther, The Prince of Peace, The
ev-er-last-ing Fa-ther, The Prince of Peace.
ev-er-last-ing Fa-ther, The Prince of Peace.
ev-er-last-ing Fa-ther, The Prince of Peace.
ev-er-last-ing Fa-ther, The Prince of Peace.
f

No. 13
PASTORAL SYMPHONY

cresc.
più cresc.
dim.
mf
B
pp
tr
cresc.
rit.

No. 14 – RECITATIVE FOR SOPRANO

"There were shepherds abiding in the field"

Luke ii: 8

RECITATIVE FOR SOPRANO

"And lo! the angel of the Lord came upon them"

Luke ii: 9

No. 15 – RECITATIVE FOR SOPRANO

"And the angel said unto them"

Luke ii: 10, 11

No. 16 – RECITATIVE FOR SOPRANO

"And suddenly there was with the angel"

Luke ii: 13

No. 17 – CHORUS
"Glory to God"

Luke ii: 14

*) Original score has here "da lontano e un poco piano" (as from a distance, and rather softly)

A
Glo - ry to God,
Glo - ry to God,
earth,
Glo - ry to God,
earth,
A
glo - - ry to God,
glo - - ry to God in the
glo - - ry to God,
glo - - ry to God in the
glo - - ry to God,
glo - - ry to God in the
high - - - est,
high - - - est,
high - - - est,
and peace on earth,
and peace on earth,

B
good - will to - - wards
good - - will to - - wards men,
good - will to - - wards men,
B
good-will to - - wards men, to-wards men, good - will
men, to-wards men, good-will to - - wards men, to - wards
to - - wards men, good - will to - wards
good - will to - wards men,
to - wards men, to - - wards men.
men, good - - will to - wards men.
men, good - - - will to - wards men.
good - - - - will to - wards men.

C
ff
Glo - ry to God, glo - - ry to God in the
Glo - ry to God, glo - - ry to God in the
Glo - ry to God, glo - - ry to God in the
Glo - ry to God, glo - - ry to God in the
C
high - - - est, and peace on earth,
high - - - est, and peace on earth,
high - - - est, and peace on earth,
high - - - est, and peace on earth,
f
p
good - will to - - wards men, to - - - - wards
good - - will to - - wards men, to - wards

D
good-will, good-will, good-will, good-will to-wards
men, good-will, good-will, good-will, good-
men, good-will, good-will, good-will, good-
good-will, good-will, good-will, good-will
D
men, good-will to-wards men.
will to-wards men, good-will to-wards men.
will to-wards men, good-will to-wards men.
to-wards men, good-will to-wards men.

No. 18 – AIR FOR SOPRANO

"Rejoice greatly, O daughter of Zion!"

Zechariah ix: 9, 10

O daughter of Zi-on! re-joice,
re-joice,
re-joice!
B
O daugh-ter of Zi-on! Re - joice great-ly,
shout,
O daugh-ter of Je-ru-sa-lem:
be-
p
f
mf

hold, thy king com-eth un - to thee, be -
mf
p
hold, thy king cometh un - to _ thee, cometh un-to thee;
f
C Meno mosso
He is _ the
p
f
p
right - - eous Sav-iour, and he shall speak
cresc.
p

peace un-to the hea - - then, he shall speak peace, he shall speak
peace, peace, he shall speak peace un-to the hea - -
D
- - then, he is___ the right - - - eous
Sav - iour, and he shall speak, he shall speak peace,
peace,___ he shall speak peace_ un-to the hea - - -
pp

E
then.
a tempo
f
Re-joice, re-
p
joice, re-joice great-ly,
f
re-joice
p
great-ly,
mf
O daugh - ter of
p
F
Zi-on!
mf
shout,
O daughter of Je-ru-sa-lem!
p
mf

Be-hold, thy king com-eth un - to thee, re-joice,
p
re-joice
mf
p
and shout, shout, shout, shout, re-joice
p
greatly,
f
G
re - joice great-ly, O daugh-ter of Zi - on! shout,
p
cresc.

— O daugh-ter of Je - - ru - sa-lem! Be-hold, thy
king com-eth un - - to thee, be-hold, thy king com-eth un - to
ad lib.
colla voce
thee.
f
p
f

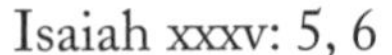

No. 19 – RECITATIVE FOR ALTO
"Then shall the eyes of the blind be opened"

Isaiah xxxv: 5, 6

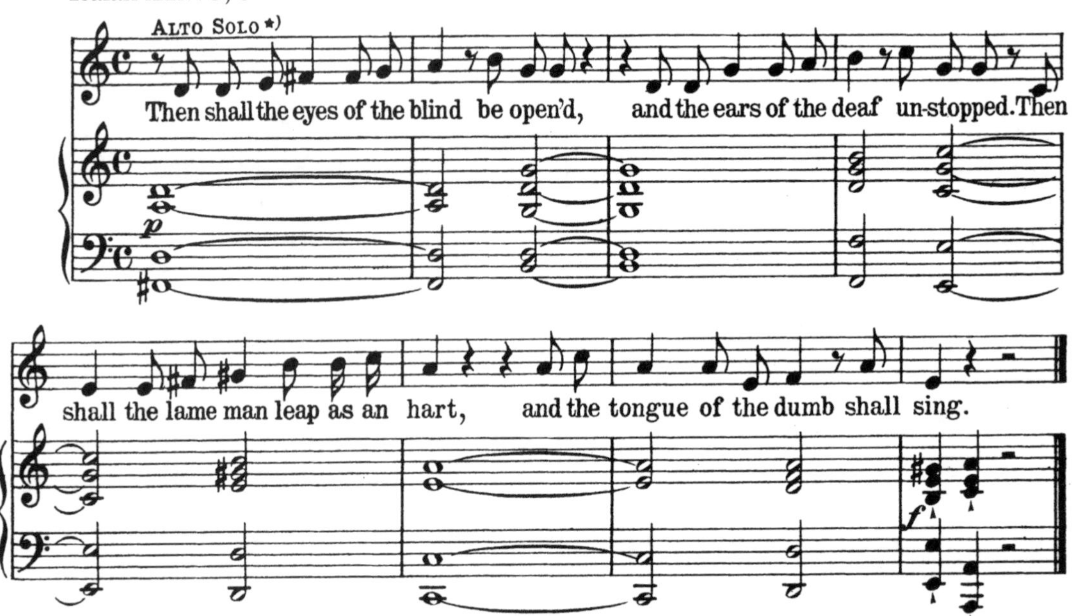

*) In the original score, this is given to the Soprano, in the key of G. But, as the first part of Nº 20 is usually sung by a Contralto, it is better that the Recitative should be sung by the same voice.

No. 20 – AIR FOR ALTO
"He shall feed His flock like a shepherd"

Isaiah xl: 11 - Matt. xi: 28, 29

*) Often sung thus: He shall feed His flock

A
*)
He shall feed His flock like a shep - - herd, and
p
He — shall ga - ther the lambs with His arm, with — His arm,
cresc.
B
and car - ry — them — in His bo - som, and
p
gen - tly lead those — that are — with young, and gen-tly lead those, — and
gen - - tly lead — those that are — with young.
mf
*) Often sung thus:
He — shall feed His flock

Soprano Solo
C
Come un - to _ Him, _ all ye that la - bour, come
un - to _ Him, ye that are _ heav-y la - den, _ and He will give you rest.
Come un - to _ Him, _ all ye that la - bour, come
un - to _ Him, ye that are heav-y la - den, _ and He _ will give you rest.
cresc.
D
Take His yoke up - on you, and learn _ of Him, for
*) Often sung thus:
Come _ un - to Him, _
**)
come _ un - to Him, _ ye that are heav-y

He — is — meek — and low - ly of heart, and ye — shall find rest, — and
ye shall find rest un - to — your souls.
E
mf
Take His yoke up-on you, and learn of Him, for He — is — meek — and
p
low - ly of heart, and ye shall find rest, and ye shall find rest un - to — your souls.
f
dim.

No. 21 – CHORUS

"His yoke is easy, and His burthen is light"

Matthew xi: 30

His yoke is ea- - - - - - - - - sy, His
ea- - - - - - - - sy, His bur-then is light, His burthen is
His yoke is
A
His burthen is
burthen is light, His bur - then is light,
light, His burthen, His bur-then, His bur - then is light, is
ea- - - - - - - sy, His bur-then, His bur - then is light,
light, His bur-then, His bur - then is light, His burthen, His
His
light, His bur-then is light,
His burthen, His bur - then is light,

bur - then is light, His yoke is ea - - -
bur - then is light, His burthen is
is light,
His yoke is ea - - - - - - - - sy,
- - - - - - sy, His bur - then is light,
light, His burthen, His bur - - then is light,
His yoke is
His bur - then is light,
His yoke is ea - - - - - - sy, His
ea - - - - - - sy, His burthen is light, His burthen, His
His

*) Original score has in bass here:

C
yoke — is ea - - - - - - - - - sy, His bur-then is light,
light, His bur-then is
light, His yoke — is ea - - - - - - - - - sy, His
C
His bur-then is light, His bur-then, His
His bur-then is light, His bur-then is light, His bur-then is
light, is light, His bur - then is
bur-then is light, is light, His bur - then is
bur-then, His bur - then, His bur-
light, His bur-then is light, His bur-
light, is light, His bur-
light, is light, His bur-

D
- - - - then is light, His yoke is ea - - - - - - - - -
- - - - then is light, His yoke is ea - sy, His yoke is
- - - - then is light, His yoke is ea - sy, is ea - - - - -
- - - - then is light, His yoke is ea - sy, is ea - - - - -
D
- sy and His bur - then is light, His yoke is ea - sy, His burthen is
ea - sy, His burthen is light, His yoke is ea - sy, His bur - then is
- sy, His burthen is light, His yoke is ea - sy, His bur - then is
- sy, His burthen is light, His yoke is ea - sy, His bur - then is
ff
light, His yoke is ea - sy, and His bur - - then is light.
light, His yoke is ea - sy, and His bur - - - then is light.
light, His yoke is ea - sy, and His bur - - - then is light.
light, His yoke is ea - sy, and His bur - - - then is light.
END OF PART I

PART II

No. 22 – CHORUS
"Behold the Lamb of God"

John i: 29

cresc.
be - hold the Lamb of God, that tak - eth a -
God, the Lamb of God, that tak - eth a -
hold the Lamb of God, the Lamb of God, that
God, be - hold the Lamb of God, that
A
way, taketh a-way the sins of the world. Be-hold the Lamb of
way the sins of the world. Be-hold the Lamb of God, the Lamb of
tak - eth a-way the sins of the world. Be-hold the Lamb of God, be -
tak - eth a-way the sins of the world.
God, the Lamb of God, of God, the Lamb of God, that tak - eth a-way the
God, be-hold the Lamb of God, the Lamb of God, that tak - eth a-way the
hold the Lamb of God, be - hold the Lamb of God, that tak - eth a-way the
Be-hold the Lamb of God, that tak - eth a-way the
*) Original score has here: and here **)

B
sins of the world, of the world. Be - hold the Lamb of God, be -
sins of the world, the sins of the world. Be - hold the Lamb of God, the
sins of the world, the sins of the world. Be - hold the Lamb of God, the
sins of the world, the sins of the world. Be - hold the Lamb of God, the
B
hold the Lamb of God, that tak - eth a - way the sins of the world,
Lamb of God, that tak - eth a - way the sins, the
Lamb of God, that tak - eth a - way the
Lamb of God, that tak - eth a - way the
mf
that tak - eth a - way
sins of the world, the sins of the world,
mf
that
sins of the world, the sins of the world,
sins of the world, the sins of the world,

C
the sins of the world,
tak-eth a-way the sins, the sins of the world, the sins of the
that tak-eth a-way the sins of the world, the sins of the
that tak-eth a-way the sins of the world, the sins of the
C
the sins of the world, that tak-eth a-way the sins of the
world, the sins of the world, that tak-eth a-way the sins of the
world, the sins of the world, that tak-eth a-way the sins of the
world, that tak-eth a-way the sins of the
world.
world.
world.
world.
*) Original score:

No. 23 – AIR FOR ALTO
"HE WAS DESPISED"

Isaiah liii: 3; l: 6

*) Original score has a♭ here, but usually a♮ is sung instead.

pis - ed and re-ject-ed of men; a man of sorrows, and acquainted with
grief, a man of sor-rows, and ac - quaint-ed with grief.
C
He was despis - ed, re-ject-ed; a man of
pp
fp
sorrows, and acquainted with grief, and acquainted with grief,
p
a man of sorrows, and ac-quainted with grief.
D
f

Fine
E
He gave His back to the
Un poco piano
Fine
smit-ers,
He gave His back to the
smit-ers,
and His cheeks to
them
that plucked
off
the
hair,
and His cheeks
to
them
that plucked
off
the

hair, and his cheeks to them that plucked off the
F
hair: He hid not His face from shame and
spit-ting, He hid not His face from shame, —
from shame, — He hid not His
face from shame, — from shame and spitting.
D. C.
p
D. C.

No. 24 – CHORUS
"Surely He hath borne our griefs"

Isaiah liii: 4, 5

*) Many editions have *f* here; according to Handel's score, *g* is correct.

borne our griefs, and car - -ried our sor - -rows,
borne our griefs, and car - -ried our sor - -rows,
borne our griefs, and car - -ried our sor - -rows,
borne our griefs, and car - -ried our sor - -rows,
sure-ly, sure-ly He hath borne our griefs, and
sure-ly, sure-ly He hath borne our griefs, and
sure-ly, sure-ly He hath borne our griefs, and
sure-ly, sure-ly He hath borne our griefs, and
car - -ried our sor - rows.
car - -ried our sor - rows. He
car - -ried our sor - rows.
car - -ried our sor - rows.
mf

A
mf
He was wound - ed for our trans - gres - sions, He was
was wound - - ed for our trans - gres - sions, He was
He was wound - ed for our trans - gres - sions, He was
He was wound - ed for our trans - gres - sions, He was
A
bruis - - ed, He was bruis - ed for our in -
bruis - - ed, He was bruis - ed for our in -
bruis - ed, He was bruis - ed for our in -
bruis - ed, He was bruis - ed for our in -
i - quities, the chas - tise - - ment, the chas -
i - quities, the chas - tise - - ment,
i - quities, the chas - tise - - ment, the chas -
i - quities, the chas - tise - - ment,
f

tise - ment of our peace
the chas - tise - ment of our peace
tise - ment of our peace
the chas - tise - ment of our peace
was up - on Him.
was up - on Him.
was up - on Him.
was up - on Him.
attacca

No. 25 – CHORUS
"And with His stripes we are healed"

Isaiah liii: 5

we — are heal - ed,
and with His stripes we are heal -
ed, and with His stripes we are heal -
with His stripes we are heal -
ed, we are heal - ed,
ed, and with His stripes we are
ed, and with His stripes we are heal - ed, we are
mf
And with His stripes we are heal -
B
f
and with His stripes we are heal -
healed,
heal - ed, and
ed, and with His stripes we are heal -
B
f

C
ed,
f
and with His stripes we are heal - - - - - - - - - -
with His stripes we are heal - - - - - - - - - - -
- - - - - - - ed, and
C
and with His stripes we are heal - - - - - - - - - -
- - - - - - - ed,
with His stripes we are heal - - - - - - - - - -
- - - - - - - - - ed,
and with His stripes
- - - - - - - - - - - - - - - - ed,
- - - - - - - - - ed,
and with His

D
and with His stripes
we are heal- - ed,
are heal- - ed, and with His
stripes we are heal- - ed,
D
we are heal- - ed, and with His
and with His stripes we are heal-
stripes we are heal- - ed,
and with His stripes we are heal- - ed,
E
stripes we are heal- - ed,
ed, and with His stripes we are
and with His stripes we are heal-
and with His stripes we are
E

heal - - - - - - - - - - - - - - -
ed, and with His stripes we are heal - -
heal - - - - - - - - - - - - ed, are heal - -
F
and with His stripes we are heal - - -
- - - - - - - - - - - ed,
- - - ed, and with His stripes we are heal - - -
- - - - - - ed, and with His
F
L.H.
Adagio
- - - - - - - - - - - - - - - ed.
and with His stripes we are heal - - - - - - ed.
- - - - - - - - - - - - - - - ed.
stripes we are heal - - - - - - - ed.
Adagio
attacca

No. 26 – CHORUS

"ALL WE LIKE SHEEP HAVE GONE ASTRAY"

Isaiah liii: 6

A
sheep; we have turn -
sheep have gone a - stray;
sheep; we have
sheep have gone a - stray;
A
- ed ev-'ry one to his own way.
we have turn -
turn - ed
- ed ev-'ry one to his own way, ev-'ry one to his own way. All we like
All we like
ev-'ry one to his own way. All we like
All we like

sheep
have gone a - stray;
sheep
have gone a - stray;
sheep
have gone a - stray;
sheep
have gone a - stray;
B
we have turn - ed,
we have turn -
B
we have turn -
- ed ev-'ry one to
we have turned, we have
- ed ev-'ry one to his own way,
we have turned ev-'ry
we have

C
his own way, to his own way, we have turn - ed
turned ev-'ry one to his own way, we have
one to his own way, we have turn - ed
turned ev-'ry one to his own way,
C
ev-'ry one to his own way; all
turn - ed ev-'ry one to his own way; all
ev-'ry one to his own way; all
we have turn - ed ev-'ry one to his own way; all
we like sheep have gone a - stray,
we like sheep have gone a - stray,
we like sheep have
we like sheep

have gone a - stray;
gone a - stray,
have gone a - stray;
D
we have turn - ed
ev - 'ry
we have turn - - ed,
we have
D
we have turn - ed,
we have
one to his own way,
we have turn - ed
we have turned, we have turn - ed
turn - - ed, we have turned,
we have

turn-ed ev-'ry one to his own way,
ev-'ry one to his own way, we have turn-ed ev-'ry
ev-'ry one to his own way, we have turn-ed ev-'ry one to his own
turn-ed ev-'ry one to his own way, we have turn-ed ev-'ry
E
we have turned ev-'ry one to his own way, to his own way; all
one to his own way, ev-'ry one to his own way; all
way, we have turned ev-'ry one to his own way; all
one, ev-'ry one to his own way, ev-'ry one to his own way; all
E
we like sheep, all we like sheep
we like sheep, all we like sheep
we like sheep, all we like sheep have gone a - stray;
we like sheep, all we like sheep have gone a - stray;

have gone a - stray;
have gone a - stray;
we have
we have turn - ed,
we have turn - ed,
we have turn - ed,
we have turn - ed,
we have
turn - ed,
we have turn - ed
F
ev-'ry one to his own way,
we have turn - ed
ev-'ry one to his own way,
we have
turn - ed
ev-'ry one to his own way,
ev-'ry one to his own way,
we have turn -
F

we have turn - - ed, we have
turn - - ed, we have turn - ed, we have turn - - ed, we have
we have turn - - ed
- ed, we have turn - ed, we have turn - -
turn - - - - - - - - ed, we have
turn - - - - - - - - - - ed, we have turn-ed
ev-'ry one to his own way, we have turn-ed
- - ed ev-'ry one to his own way, we have
turn-ed ev-'ry one to his own way, we have turn-ed ev-'ry one to
ev-'ry one to his own way, we have turn-ed ev-'ry one to
ev-'ry one to his own way, we have turn-ed ev-'ry one to
turn-ed ev-'ry one to his own way, we have turn-ed ev-'ry one to

G
Adagio
mf
his own way; and the Lord hath laid on
his own way; and the
his own way; and the Lord hath
f
his own way; and the Lord hath laid on Him,
Adagio (♩ = 60)
cresc.
Him, and the Lord hath laid on Him, hath laid on Him,
Lord hath laid on Him, on Him, hath
laid on Him, on Him, hath
the Lord hath laid on Him
p
dim.
on Him the in - i - qui - ty of us all.
laid on Him the in - i - qui - ty of us all.
laid on Him the in - i - qui - ty of us all.
the in - i - qui - ty of us all.

No. 27 – RECITATIVE FOR TENOR

"All they that see Him, laugh Him to scorn"

Psalm xxii: 7

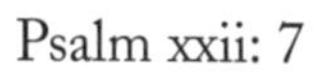

No. 28 – CHORUS
"He trusted in God that He would deliver Him"

Psalm xxii: 8

A
He trust - ed in
let him de-liv-er him, if he de-light in him, if he de -
he de-light in him, if he de-light in him, if he de-light in
A
God that he would de - liv-er him; let him de-liv-er him, if he de -
light in him, let him de - liv-er him; if he de-light in him, if he de -
him.
He trust - ed in God that he would de-liv-er him;
light in him, if he de - light
light in him, if he de - light
He trust - ed in God, in God, in God he trust - ed; let him de-liv-er

let him de-liv-er him, if he de-light in him,
in him,
in — him let him de-liv-er him,
him, if he de-light in him, if he de-light in him, let him de-
mf
mf
B
let him de-liv-er him, if he de-light in him,
let him de-liv-er him, if he de-light in him,
if he de-light in him, if he de-
liv-er him. He trust-ed in
f
He trust-ed in God that he would de-liv-er him; let him de-
light in — him, let him de-liv-er him, if he de-
God, he trust-ed in God; let him de-liv-er him, if he de-

let him de - liv - er him. He
li - ver him, if he de - light in him, if he de - light
light in him, if he de - light in him. He trust - ed in God, he
light in him, if he de - light in him,
trust - ed in God that he would de - liv - er him; let him de - liv - er him,
in him, let him de - liv - er him, if he de - light in
trust - ed in God; let him de - liv - er him, if he de - light in
C
if he de - light in him, let him de - liv - er him,
him, if he de - light in him, let him de - liv - er him,
him, if he de - light in him, let him de - liv - er him,
let him de - liv - er him, let him de -
C

if he de - light in him, if he de -
let him de - liv - er him, if he de - light in
He trust - ed in God that he would de - liv - er
liv - er him,
light in him, let him de - liv - er him, if he de-light in him, let
him; let him de - liv - er him, if he de -
him; let him de - liv - er him, if he de-light in him, let
let him de-liv - er him.
D
him de - liv - er him,
light in him. He trust - ed in God, let him de - liv - er him, if he de -
him de - liv - er him. He trust - ed in God, let him de - liv - er him, if he de-light
He trust - ed in God, that he would de - liv - er him;
D

mf
let him de - liv - er him,
light in him, let him de - liv - er him,
in him, let him de -
let him de-liv - er him, if he de-light in him,
let him de-liv - er him, let him de-liv - er him.
if he de - light in
liv - er him, if he de-light in
mf
let him de - liv - er him, if he de-light in
E
He trust - ed in God that he would de - liv - er him; let him de -
f
him. He trust - ed in God; let him de - liv - er him, if he de - light
f
him, if he de-light,
f
him, if he de-light in him, if he de -
E

liv - er him, if he de - light in him,
in him, let him de - liv - er him, let him de - liv - er him, if he de -
if he de - light in him, let him de - liv - er him,
light in him, let him de - liv - er him.
if he de - light in him, if he de - light
light
if he de - light in him, if he de - light
He trust - ed in God, that he would de -
Adagio
in him, let him de - liv - er him, if he de - light in him.
in him, let him de - liv - er him, if he de - light in him.
in him, let him, let him de - liv - er him, if he de - light in him.
liv - er him; let him, let him de - liv - er him, if he de - light in him.
Adagio

No. 29 – RECITATIVE FOR TENOR

"Thy rebuke hath broken His heart"

Psalm lxix: 20

No. 30 – AIR FOR TENOR

"Behold, and see if there be any sorrow"

Lamentations i: 12

No. 31 – RECITATIVE FOR TENOR

"He was cut off out of the land of the living"

Isaiah liii: 8

No. 32 – AIR FOR TENOR

"But Thou didst not leave His soul in hell"

Psalm xvi: 10

*) This is according to Handel's score; other editions have not the appoggiatura: land

soul in hell, nor didst Thou suf-fer, nor didst Thou suf-fer Thy
Ho - ly One to see cor-rup - tion.
B
tr
f
But Thou didst not leave His
p
soul in hell, Thou didst not leave, Thou didst not leave His
soul in hell, nor didst Thou suf - fer Thy

C
Ho - ly One to see cor-rup-tion, nor didst Thou suf-fer, nor
cresc.
p
didst Thou suf-fer Thy Ho - ly One to see cor - rup - tion,
cresc.
nor didst Thou suf-fer, nor didst Thou suf-fer Thy Ho-ly One, Thy
tr
p
D
Ho-ly One to see cor-rup-tion.
f

No. 33 – CHORUS

"Lift up your heads, O ye gates"

Psalm xxiv: 7-10

*) Handel's score has here, and in all similar cases, "this" King, not "the" King. It has become traditional, however, to sing "the" King.

this
the King of glo - ry? who is the King of glo - ry? who
this
this
the King of glo - ry? who is the King of glo - ry? who
this
mf
The Lord strong and might-y, the Lord strong and might-y, the Lord
mf
The Lord strong and might-y, the Lord strong and might-y, the Lord
mf
The Lord strong and might-y, the Lord strong and might-y, the Lord
this
is the King of glo-ry?
this
is the King of glo-ry?

B
might - y in bat-tle.
might - y in bat-tle.
mf
might - y in bat-tle. Lift up your heads, O ye_ gates, and be ye lift up, ye
Lift up your heads, O ye_ gates, and be ye lift up, ye
Lift up your heads, O ye gates, and be ye lift up, ye
B
mf
ev - er-last-ing doors, and the King_ of glo - ry shall come in,__ and the
ev - er-last-ing doors, and the King of glo - ry shall come in, and the
ev - er-last-ing doors, and the King_ of glo - ry shall come in,__ and the

Who is the King of glo-ry? who
this
King of glo-ry shall come in.
King of glo-ry shall come in.
is the King of glo-ry? who is the King of glo-ry?
The Lord of hosts,
The Lord of hosts,
The Lord of hosts,

SOPRANO I II
C
The Lord of hosts, He is the King of glo-ry, He
ALTO
The Lord of hosts, He is the King of glo-ry, He
TENOR
the Lord of hosts, He is the King of glo-ry, He
BASS
the Lord of hosts, He is the King of glo-ry, He
C
is the King of glo-ry, He is the King of glo-ry, He is the King of
is the King of glo-ry, He is the King of glo-ry, He is the King of glo-ry, He
is the King of glo-ry, He is the King of glo-ry, He is the King of glo-ry, He
is the King of glo-ry, He is the King of glo-ry,
glo-ry, He is the King of glo-ry, He is the King— of glo-
is the King of glo-ry, the Lord of hosts, He is the King of glo-
is the King of glo-ry, the Lord of hosts, He is the King of glo-
the Lord of hosts, He is the King of glo-

D
- - - - - ry, the Lord of hosts, He is the King of glo - - -
- - - - - ry, the Lord of hosts, He is the King of
ry, the Lord of hosts, He is the King of
- - - - - - ry,
D
- - - - - - - - - - - ry,
glo - - - - - - - ry, of glo - ry, the Lord of
glo - - - - - - - - - ry,
the Lord of hosts, He is the King of glo -
hosts, He is the King of glo - - ry, of glo -
the Lord of hosts, He is the King of glo - - ry, of glo - - -
the Lord of hosts, He is the King of glo - - ry, of glo -

ry, He
ry, He
ry, of glo ry, He
ry, He
E
is the King of glo-ry, He is the King of glo-ry, the Lord of hosts,
is the King of glo-ry, He is the King of glo-ry, the Lord of
is the King of glo-ry, He is the King of glo-ry, the Lord of
is the King of glo-ry, He is the King of glo-ry, the Lord of
E
the Lord of hosts, the Lord of hosts, the Lord of hosts, He
hosts, the Lord of hosts, the Lord of hosts, the Lord of
hosts, the Lord of hosts, the Lord of hosts, the Lord of
hosts, the Lord of hosts, the Lord of hosts, the Lord of

is the King of glo -
hosts, He is the King of glo - ry, of
hosts, He is the King of glo - ry, of
hosts, He is the King of glo -
ry, He is the King of glo - ry, He is the King of glo - ry,
glo - ry, He is the King of glo - ry, He is the King of glo - ry,
glo - ry, He is the King of glo - ry, He is the King of glo - ry,
ry, He is the King of glo - ry, He is the King of glo - ry,
F
cresc.
the Lord of hosts, the Lord of hosts, the Lord of
the Lord of hosts, the Lord of hosts, the Lord of hosts, He
the Lord of hosts, the Lord of hosts, the Lord of hosts, He
the Lord of hosts, the Lord of hosts, the Lord of

ff
hosts, He is the King of glo - - - - - - - - - -
is the King, the King of glo - - - - - - - - - - -
is the King of glo - ry, the King of glo - - - - - - - -
hosts, He is the King of glo - - - - - - - - - - -
- - ry, the King of glo - ry, He is the King of glo - ry, He
- - ry, the King of glo - ry, He is the King of glo - ry, He
- - ry, the King of glo - ry, He is the King of glo - ry, He
- - ry, the King of glo - ry, He is the King of glo - ry, He
is the King of glo - ry, of glo - - ry.
is the King of glo - ry, of glo - - ry.
is the King of glo - ry, of glo - - ry.
is the King of glo - ry, of glo - - ry.

*) No. 34 – RECITATIVE FOR TENOR
"Unto which of the angels said He"

Hebrews i: 5

*) No. 35 – CHORUS
"Let all the angels of God worship Him"

Hebrews i: 6

*) Generally omitted

Him, let all the an - gels of
Him, let all the an - - gels of
Him,
Him,
God, let all the an - - - - gels of God wor - ship
God wor - - - - - - - - - ship
let all the an - gels of God wor - - - - ship
A
Him, let all the
Him, let all the an - gels of God
let all the an - - - - - gels of God
Him, let
A

an - - - gels of God wor - - ship Him,
wor - ship Him,
wor - - - - - - - - - - - - - ship
all the an - gels of God wor - - - - - - ship
let all the an - - - - - - gels of God wor - ship
let all the an - gels of
Him, let all the an - gels of God wor - ship Him,
Him, let all the an - - - -
Him,
God wor - - - - ship Him, let all the
let all the an - - - - gels of God wor -
- - - - - - gels of God wor - - - - - - -

B
let all the an -
an - gels of God wor - ship Him,
- ship Him, let all the an - gels of God
- ship Him,
B
- gels of God wor -
wor -
wor -
C
- ship Him, let all the an -
- ship Him, let all the an -
- ship Him, let all the an -
let all the an -
C

- gels of God, let all the an - gels of
- gels of God, let all the an - gels of
- gels of God, let all the an - gels of
God wor - ship
God wor - ship
God wor - ship
- gels of God wor - ship
Him.
Him.
Him.
Him.

*) No. 36 – AIR FOR BASS
"Thou art gone up on high"

Psalm lxviii: 18

*) Generally omitted

e - - ven for Thine en - - - - - - e-mies,
yea, e - ven for Thine en-e-mies,
B
f
that the Lord
p
God might dwell a-mong them, that the Lord God might dwell,

C
might dwell a-mong them.
f
Thou art gone up on high, Thou art gone up on high, Thou hast
p
led cap-tiv - i - ty cap-tive, Thou hast led cap-tiv - i - ty cap-tive,
and re - ceiv - ed gifts for men; yea, e - - ven
p
for Thine en - - - - - - - - - - -
tr

D
-e-mies, for Thine en-e-mies,
that the Lord God might dwell a-mong them,
that the Lord God might dwell
a-mong them,
E
that the Lord God, that the Lord

God might dwell a- - mong them, might dwell
a-mong
F
them, that the Lord God might dwell a-mong them.
f

No. 37 – CHORUS
"The Lord gave the word"

Psalm lxviii: 11

-pa-ny of the preach-ers,
com-pa-ny, the com-pa-ny of the preach-ers,
com- -pa-ny of the preach-ers,
-pa-ny of the preach-ers,
A
great was the com-pa-ny of the preachers. The Lord gave the word;
great was the com-pa-ny of the preachers. The Lord gave the word;
great was the com-pa-ny of the preachers.
great was the com-pa-ny of the preachers.
A
great was the com- -pa-ny, the com-
great was the com- -pa-ny, the com-
Great was the com-pa-ny, the com- -pa-ny, the
Great was the com-pa-ny, the com- -pa-ny, the
Ped.

- pa - ny, the com - - - - - - - pa - ny of the preach -
- pa - ny, the com - pa - ny of the preach - - ers, of the preach -
com - - - - - - pa - ny of the preach - - ers, of the preach -
com - - - - - - - - - - - - pa - ny of the preach -
B
ers, great was the com - pa - ny of the preach-ers,
ers, great was the com - - - - - - - - -
ers, great was the com - pa - ny of the preach-ers,
ers, great was the com - - pa - ny, the com - - - -
B
great was the com - pa - ny of the preach-ers, of the preach-ers,
- pa - ny, the com - - - - - - - - - - - pa - ny, the
great was the com - pa - ny of the preach-ers, the com - - - -
- - - - - - pa - ny, the com - - - - - - - - -

great was the com - - - - - - - - - - - - - -
com - - - - - - pa-ny, the com - pa-ny, the com - - - - -
- - - - - - - pa-ny, the com - - - - - - pa-ny, the
- - pa-ny, the com - - - - - - - pa-ny, the com - - - -
- - - - - - - pa-ny of the preach - - ers, of the preach-
- - pa-ny, the com-pa-ny of the preach - - ers, of the preach-
com - - - - - pa-ny of the preach - - ers, of the preach-
- - - - - - - pa-ny of the preach - - ers, of the preach-
ers.
ers.
ers.
ers.

No. 38 – AIR FOR SOPRANO
"How beautiful are the feet of them"

Romans x: 15

preach the gos-pel of peace, and bring glad ti- - -dings, and
bring glad ti- - -dings, glad ti - dings of good things, and
B
bring glad ti- -dings, glad tidings of good things, and bring glad tidings, glad
ti-dings of good things, glad tidings of good things!

No. 39 – CHORUS
"Their sound is gone out into all lands"

Romans x: 18

their sound is gone out in - to all lands, their sound is gone
their sound is gone out, is gone out, their sound is gone
out in - to all lands, in - to all
out in - to all lands,
out in - to all lands,
out, is gone out in - to all lands,
lands, in - to all lands,
their sound is gone out in - to all lands,
A
f
and their
f
and their words un - to the ends of the world,
A

words un - to the ends of the world,
un - to the ends of the world,
and their
un - to the ends of the world,
and their
un - to the ends of the world,
words un - to the ends of the world,
un-to the ends of the
words un-to the ends of the world, un - to the ends of the
un-to the ends of the world, of the
and their words, and their words un - to the ends of the

B
world; their sound is gone out, is gone out in - to all
world; their sound is gone out, is gone out in - to all
world; their sound is gone out in - to all
world; their sound is gone out in - to all
B
lands, and their words un - to the ends of the
lands, and their words un - to the ends of the
lands, and their words, and their words un - to the ends of the
lands, and their
world, and their
world, and their
world, of the world, and their
words un - to the ends of the world,
Ped.
*

words un - to the ends of the world, and their
words un - to the ends of the world,
words, and their words un - to the ends of the
and their words un - to the ends of the
cresc.
words un-to the ends of the world,
cresc.
and their words un - to the ends of the
world,
cresc.
and their
world,
cresc.
and their words un-to the ends of the world,
un - to the ends of the world.
world, un - to the ends of the world.
words un - to the ends of the world, un-to the ends of the world.
un - to the ends, un - to the ends of the world.

No. 40 – AIR FOR BASS

"Why do the nations so furiously rage together?"

Psalm ii: 1, 2

A BASS SOLO
Why do the na - - - - tions so
fu - rious - ly rage to - - geth - er? why
do the peo - ple im - a - gine a vain
thing? Why do the na - - - tions
p

rage
so
fu-rious-ly to-geth-er?
why
do the peo-ple im-a-
-gine a vain

thing? im - a - - - - - - - - -
- gine a vain thing?
B
Why do the na - tions so fu - riously rage to -
geth - - er, and why do the
peo - ple, and why do the

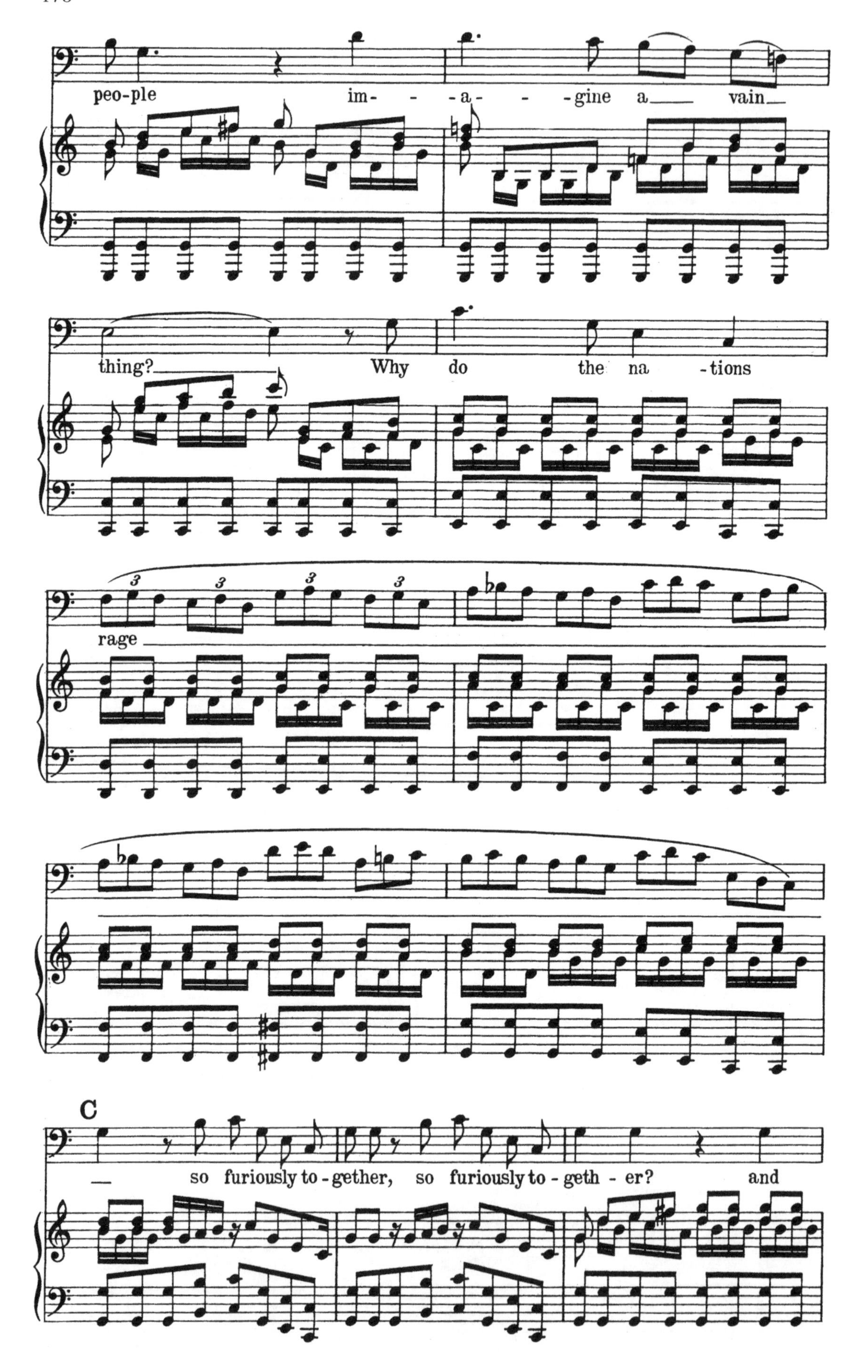
peo-ple im- - -a- - -gine a vain
thing? Why do the na -tions
rage
C
so furiously to-gether, so furiously to-geth - er? and

why do the peo-ple im- - a- - gine a vain
thing? im - a- - - - - - - - -
cresc.
f
- gine a vain thing? and
p
why do the peo-ple im- - a - gine a vain
D
thing?
f

E
The kings of the earth rise up, and the
p
rul - - ers take coun - sel to - geth - - er, take
coun - - - - - - - - - - - - - - - - -
- - - - - - - - - - - sel, take

coun - - sel to - geth - er against the Lord, and a -
gainst His an - oint - - - - - - - - - - -
- - - - - - - - - - - - - - -
- - - ed, a - gainst the Lord and His an -
oint - - - - - - - - - - - - - ed.

No. 41 – CHORUS

"Let us break their bonds asunder"

Psalm ii: 3

A
let us break their bonds a - sun - der,
let us break their bonds a - sun - der,
let us break their bonds a - sun - der, and cast a - way
let us break their bonds a - sun - der,
A
and cast a - - way
their yokes from us, and cast a -
and cast a - - way
their yokes from us, and cast a - way their yokes from
way their yokes from us, and cast a - way their yokes from

their yokes from us, and cast a - way their yokes from
us, and cast a - way, and cast a - way their yokes from
us, and cast a - way, and cast a - way their yokes from
f
and cast a - - way,
us, and cast a - way their yokes from us. Let us break their
us, and cast a - way their yokes from us.
us, and cast a - way their yokes from us. Let us break their bonds,
and cast a - way their yokes from us.
B
bonds, let us break their bonds,
Let us break their bonds a - sun - der, let us break their bonds,
let us break their bonds a -
Let us break their bonds a - sun-der, let us break their

let us break their bonds a - sun - der, let us break their bonds a -
let us break their bonds a - sun - der,
sun - der, let us break their bonds, let us break their
bonds, let us break their bonds a - sun - der,
sun - der, let us, let us break, let us break their bonds a -
let us break their bonds, let us break their
bonds a - sun - der, let us break, let us break their bonds,
let us break their bonds a - sun - der,
sun - der, their bonds a - sun - der, and cast a - way
bonds, their bonds a - sun - der,
let us break their bonds a - sun - der, and cast a - way,
let us break their bonds a - sun - der,
C
f

their yokes from
and cast a - way,
and cast a - - way
us, and cast a - way their yokes from us, and cast a -
and cast a - - way
and cast a - way their yokes from us, and cast a -
their yokes, their yokes from us, and cast a -
way their yokes from us.
their yokes from us.
way their yokes from us. Let us break their bonds a -
way their yokes from us. Let us break their
R.H.

ff
Let us break their bonds a - - sun - der, and cast a - -
ff
Let us break their bonds, and cast
ff
sun - - der, and cast, and cast a - -
ff
bonds, and cast a - - way their yokes from
ff
way,
a - way their yokes, their yokes from us, and cast a - -
way, and cast a - way their yokes from us, and cast a - -
us, and cast a - way their yokes from us, and cast a - -
D
— and cast a - - way their yokes from us,
way, and cast a - - way their yokes, let us break their
way, and cast a - - way their yokes, let us break their bonds a -
way, and cast a - - way their yokes from us,
D

let us break their bonds, and cast a- -way, and cast a-
bonds, their bonds a- -sun- -der, and cast a- -way, and cast a-
sun- -der, their bonds a- -sun- -der, and cast a- -way, and cast a-
let us break their bonds a- -sun- -der, and cast a- -way, and cast a-
way their yokes from us.
way their yokes from us.
way their yokes from us.
way their yokes from us.

No. 42 – RECITATIVE FOR TENOR

"HE THAT DWELLETH IN HEAVEN"

Psalm ii: 4

No. 43 – AIR FOR TENOR

"THOU SHALT BREAK THEM"

Thou shalt dash them in piec - es like a pot - - ter's
ves - sel, Thou shalt dash them in piec - es, in
cresc.
piec - es like a pot - - - - - - - - -
p
B
- - ter's ves - sel.
f
Thou shalt break them,

Thou shalt break them with a rod
of i - ron; Thou shalt
dash them in piec-es like a pot - - - - - ter's
C
ves - sel, Thou shalt dash them in piec-es like a
pot - - - - - - - - - ter's ves - sel, like a
mf
p
f
p
*)Handel in his score has this section in unison

pot - - ter's ves - sel,
Thou shalt dash them in
piec - es
like a pot - - - - - - ter's
D
ves - sel.
f
f

No. 44 – CHORUS
"Hallelujah!"

Rev. xix: 6; xi: 15; xix: 16

*) Handel's score has here

**)

*) Handel's score has one 8th note e here only; see foot-note on next page.

*) Handel's score has here (jah, Hal-le) 2 syllables for one note, it is therefore better to substitute two 16th notes for the 8th

(p)
C
le - - lu - -jah! The king-dom of this
Hal - le - lu - jah! The king-dom of this
le - - - lu - jah! The king-dom of this
lu - jah! Hal-le - lu - jah! The king-dom of this
(p)
mf
f
world is be - - come the King - dom of our
world is be - - come the King - dom of our
world is be - - come the King - dom of our
world is be - - come the King - dom of our
D
Lord and of His Christ, and of His Christ;
Lord and of His Christ, and of His Christ;
Lord and of His Christ, and of His Christ;
Lord and of His Christ, and of His Christ; and He shall reign for ev - er and

and He shall reign for ev - - er and ev - - -
ev - er, for ev - er and ev - - er, and He shall
and He shall reign for ev - - er and
er, and He shall reign for ev - - er and
reign, and He shall reign for ev - er, for
and He shall reign for ev - er and ev - -
ev - - er, for ev-er and ev-er, for ev - er and
ev - - er, and He shall reign for ev-er and
ev-er, for ev-er, for ev-er and ev-er, for ev - er, for ev-er and

E
er. King of Kings,
ev - er. King of Kings,
ev - er, for ev - er and ev - er. Hal - le - lu - jah! Hal - le -
ev - er, for ev - er and ev - er. Hal - le - lu - jah! Hal - le -
E
and Lord of Lords.
and Lord of Lords.
lu - jah! For ev - er and ev - er. Hal - le - lu - jah! Hal - le -
lu - jah! For ev - er and ev - er. Hal - le - lu - jah! Hal - le
King of Kings,
For ev - er and ev - er. Hal - le - lu - jah! Hal - le -
lu - jah! For ev - er and ev - er. Hal - le - lu - jah! Hal - le -
lu - jah! For ev - er and ev - er. Hal - le - lu - jah! Hal - le -

and Lord of Lords,
lu-jah! For ev-er and ev-er. Hal-le-lu-jah! Hal-le-
lu-jah! For ev-er and ev-er. Hal-le-lu-jah! Hal-le-
lu-jah! For ev-er and ev-er. Hal-le-lu-jah! Hal-le-
King of Kings,
lu-jah! For ev-er and ev-er. Hal-le-lu-jah! Hal-le-
lu-jah! For ev-er and ev-er. Hal-le-lu-jah! Hal-le-
lu-jah! For ev-er and ev-er. Hal-le-lu-jah! Hal-le-
ff
F
f
and Lord of Lords, and Lord of Lords, and He shall
lu-jah! King of Kings, and Lord of Lords,
lu-jah! King of Kings, and Lord of Lords,
lu-jah! King of Kings, and Lord of Lords, and He shall

reign,
and
and He shall
reign,
and He shall
and He shall reign, and He
shall
reign,
reign
for
ev-
-er
and
ev-
-er,
He shall reign for
ev-er and ev-
-er,
reign
for ev-er and ev-
-er, King of
and He shall reign
for ev-er and ev-
-er, King of
and He shall reign for ev-er and ev-er, King of
for ev-er and ev-er.
Hal-le-lu-jah! Hal-le-
Kings, for ev-er and ev-er, and Lord of Lords. Hal-le-lu-jah! Hal-le-
Kings, and Lord of Lords,
Kings, for ev-er and ev-er, and Lord of Lords. Hal-le-lu-jah! Hal-le-

lu-jah! and He shall reign for ev- - er, for
lu-jah! and He shall reign for
and He shall reign for ev- - er, for
lu-jah! and He shall reign for ev- - er, for
G
ev-er and ev- - er, King of Kings, and Lord of
ev-er and ev- - er, King of Kings, and Lord of
ev-er and ev- - er, King of Kings, and Lord of
ev-er and ev- - er, King of Kings, and Lord of
G
Lords, King of Kings, and Lord of Lords, and
Lords, King of Kings, and Lord of Lords, and
Lords, King of Kings, and Lord of Lords, and
Lords, King of Kings, and Lord of Lords, and He shall

END OF PART II

PART III

No. 45 – AIR FOR SOPRANO

"I know that my Redeemer liveth"

Job xix: 25, 26; 1 Cor. xv: 20

*) This appoggiatura is not in Handel's score

stand at the lat - - - ter day up - on the earth,
up - on the earth:
f
p
cresc.
D
And though worms de - stroy this bod - y,
f
tr
p
yet in my flesh shall I see

God, yet in my flesh shall I_ see God.
E
I know that my Re-
deem-er liv-eth. And though worms de - stroy this
bod-y, yet in my flesh shall I see God, yet in my
flesh ___ shall I see God, shall I see God. I

know that my Re - deem - er liv - eth.
F
For now is Christ ris - en from the dead,
f
p
pp
the first - - fruits of them that
sleep, of them that sleep, the
G
first - - fruits of them that sleep.
p

cresc.
For now is Christ ris-en, for now is Christ
p
cresc.
ris-en from the dead,
p
the
Adagio
first-fruits of them, of them that sleep.
f

No. 46 – CHORUS

"Since by man came death"

1 Cor. xv: 21

dead, by man came al - so the re - sur - - rec - tion of the
dead, by man came al - so the re - - sur - rec - tion of the
dead, by man came al - so the re - sur - - rec - tion of the
dead, by man came al - so the re - sur - - rec - tion of the
dead, by man came al - so the re - sur - - rec - tion of the dead.
dead, by man came al - so the re - sur - - rec - tion of the dead.
dead, by man came al - so the re - sur - - rec - tion of the dead.
dead, by man came al - so the re - sur - - rec - tion of the dead.

B Grave
p
For as in Ad - am all die, for as in Ad - am all die,
For as in Ad - am all die, for as in Ad - am all die,
For as in Ad - am all die, for as in Ad - am all die,
For as in Ad - am all die, for as in Ad - am all die,
B Grave (𝅗𝅥=60)
C Allegro
f
e - ven so in Christ shall all be made a - live, e - ven so in
e - ven so in Christ shall all be made a - live, e - ven so in
e - ven so in Christ shall all be made a - live, e - ven so in
e - ven so in Christ shall all be made a - live, e - ven so in
C Allegro (𝅗𝅥=84)
Christ shall all be made a - live, e - ven so in Christ shall all,
Christ shall all be made a - live, e - ven so in Christ shall all,
Christ shall all be made a - live, e - ven so in Christ shall all,
Christ shall all be made a - live, e - ven so in Christ shall all,

— so in Christ shall all — be made a - live, ev'n so in
— so in Christ shall all — be made a - - live, ev'n so in
— so in Christ shall all be made a - live, ev'n so in
— so in Christ shall all — be made a - live, ev'n so in
Christ shall all, shall all be — made a - live.
Christ shall all, shall all be made a - live.
Christ shall all, shall all be — made a - live.
Christ shall all, shall all be made a - live.

No. 47 – RECITATIVE FOR BASS

"Behold, I tell you a mystery"

1 Cor. xv: 51, 52

No. 48 – AIR FOR BASS

"The trumpet shall sound"

1 Cor. xv: 52, 53

BASS SOLO
A
The trum-pet shall sound,
and the dead shall be
raised,
and the dead shall be raised in-cor-
rup-ti-ble;
the
f
p

B
trum-pet shall sound,
and the dead shall be
raised,
be raised in-cor-rup-ti-ble,
be
raised in-cor-rup-ti-ble,
and we shall be chang'd,
and we shall be chang'd.
C
*) Handel's score has here
in-cor-rup-ti-ble
**) Handel's score has here, including last note in preceding bar,
in-cor-rup-ti-ble

Trumpet
The trum-pet shall sound, the
trum-pet shall sound,
D
and the dead shall be raised,
be raised in-cor-rup-ti-ble,
be raised in-cor-rup-ti-ble,
and
mf
f
p

we shall be chang'd, be chang'd,
and we shall be chang'd,
E
f
and we shall be chang'd,
we
p
shall be chang'd,
we shall be
F
chang'd,
and we shall be chang'd,

and we shall be
chang'd, we shall be chang'd,
Adagio G a tempo
and we shall be chang'd, we shall be chang'd.
f a tempo
Fine

*) This section is generally omitted.

tal - - - - - - - - - - - - - -
- - - - - - - - - - i - ty, and this
mor - tal must put on im - mor - tal - - - - -
- - - - - - - - - - - - - - -
- - - - i - ty, im - mor - tal - - i - ty. The
Dal 𝄋
Dal 𝄋

*) No. 49 – RECITATIVE FOR ALTO

"THEN SHALL BE BROUGHT TO PASS"

1 Cor. xv: 54

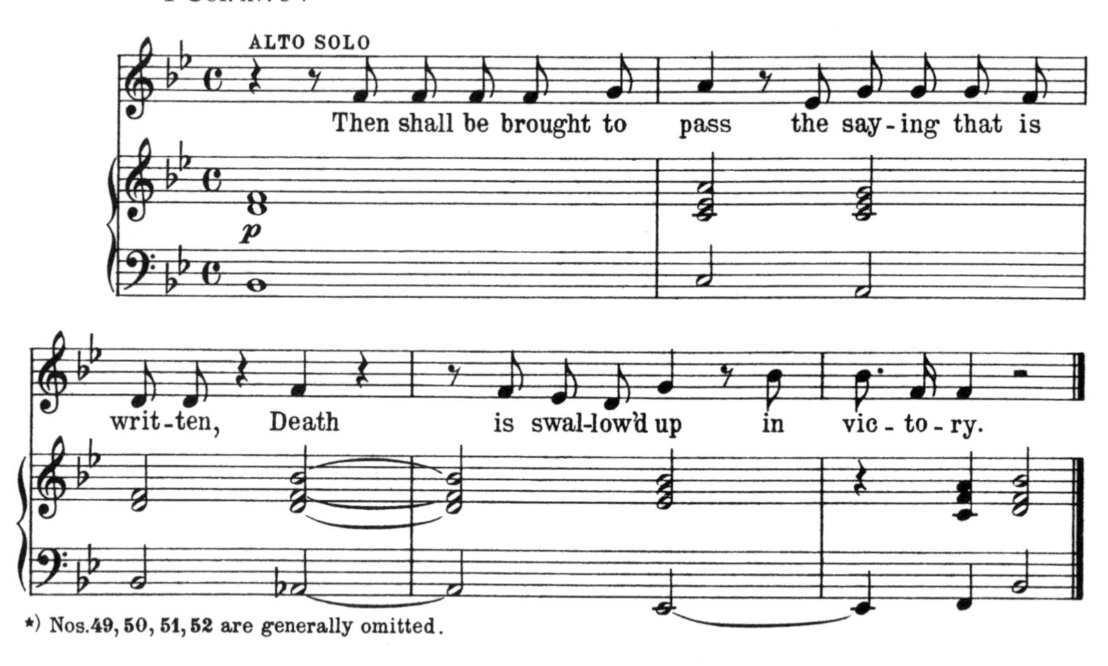

*) Nos. 49, 50, 51, 52 are generally omitted.

*) No. 50 – DUET FOR ALTO AND TENOR

"O DEATH, WHERE IS THY STING?"

1 Cor. xv: 55, 56

N.B. – This Duet is given in the abridged form indicated by Handel in the Dublin score. Compare the Full Score.

death, O death, where, where is thy sting? where, O grave, where is thy
where, where is thy sting? where, where is thy sting? O grave, where is thy
A
vic-to-ry? O death, where, where is thy sting? O grave,
vic-to-ry? O grave! O death, where, where is thy sting? O
A
O grave, where is thy vic-to-ry? O grave, where is thy
grave, O grave, where is thy vic-to-ry? O grave, where is thy

vic-to-ry? The sting of death is sin, the sting of death is sin, and
vic-to-ry? The sting of death is sin, and the
the strength of sin is the law, the sting
strength of sin is the law, the sting of death is sin, the
of death is sin, and the strength of sin is the law.
sting of death is sin, and the strength of sin is the law.
attacca

No. 51 – CHORUS
"But thanks be to God"

1 Cor. xv: 57

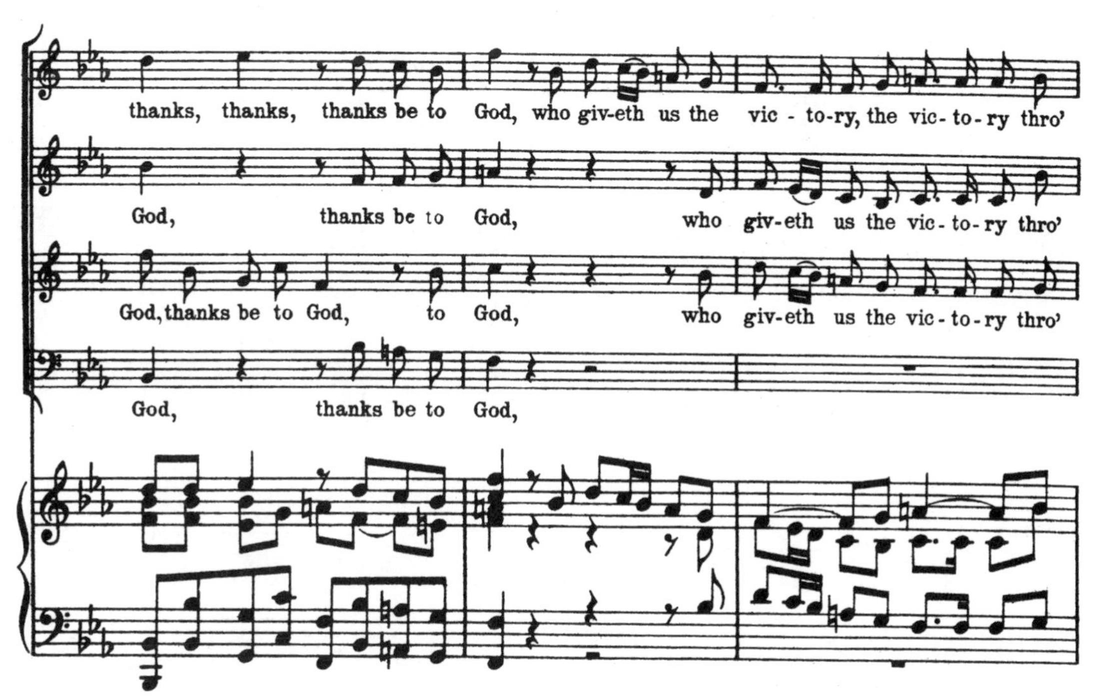

our Lord Je - sus Christ,
our Lord Je - sus Christ, who giv - eth us the
our Lord Je - sus Christ, who giv - eth us the vic - to - ry, who
who giv - eth us the vic - to - ry, the vic - to - ry thro'
A
who giv - eth us the vic - to - ry thro' our Lord Je - sus Christ,
vic - to - ry, who giv - eth us the vic - to - ry thro' our Lord Je - sus Christ, but
giv - eth us, who giv - eth us the vic - to - ry thro' our Lord Je - sus Christ,
our Lord Je - - sus Christ, thro' our Lord Je - sus Christ,
A
but
thanks, but thanks, thanks be to God, thanks be to God,
but thanks, but thanks, thanks,

thanks, but thanks, but thanks, but thanks, thanks be to God,
thanks be to God, but thanks, thanks be to
thanks be to God, to God, thanks be to God, to God,
but thanks, but thanks, but thanks be to God, thanks
thanks be to God, but thanks, but thanks, thanks,
God, to God, but thanks be to God,
but thanks be to God, but
be to God, but thanks, but thanks, thanks be to God,
B
thanks, thanks be to God, thanks, thanks be to God, thanks be to
thanks, but thanks, thanks, thanks be to God, thanks be to God, to
B

God, who giv-eth us the vic - to-ry, the
who giv-eth us the vic - to-ry, who giv-eth us the
God, who giv-eth us the vic-to-ry, who giv-eth us the
who giv-eth us the
C
vic - to-ry thro' our Lord Je - sus Christ, but thanks be to God, but thanks,
vic - to-ry thro' our Lord Je - sus Christ, but thanks, thanks be to God, but
vic - to-ry thro' our Lord Je - sus Christ, but thanks be to God, but
vic - to-ry thro' our Lord Je - sus Christ, but thanks be to God, but
C
but thanks, thanks be to God, to God, who giv-eth us the
thanks, but thanks, thanks be to God,
thanks, but thanks, thanks be to God, who
thanks, but thanks, thanks be to God, who

vic - to - ry, who giv - eth us the vic - to - ry, who giv - eth us the
who giv - eth us the vic - to - ry, the
giv - eth us the vic - to - ry, the vic - to - ry, who giv - eth us the
giv - eth us the vic - to - ry, the vic - to - ry, who giv - eth us the
D
vic - to - ry thro' our Lord Je - sus Christ,
vic - to - ry thro' our Lord Je - sus Christ, but thanks, but thanks, thanks,
vic - to - ry thro' our Lord Je - sus Christ, but thanks, thanks, thanks be to
vic - to - ry thro' our Lord Je - sus Christ,
D
but thanks, thanks, thanks be to
thanks be to God, thanks, thanks be to God, but thanks, thanks,
God, thanks, thanks be to God, to God, but thanks, thanks,
but thanks, thanks,

God, thanks be to God, who giv-eth us the vic - - to -
thanks be to God, to God, who
thanks be to God, thanks be to God, who giv-eth us the
thanks be to God, thanks be to God, who
- ry thro' our Lord Je - - - sus Christ, who
giv - eth us the vic - to - ry, who giv - eth us the vic - to - ry, who
vic - to - ry, who giv - eth us the vic - to - ry, the vic - to - ry, who
giv - eth us the vic - to - ry, who giv - eth us the vic - to - ry, who
Adagio
giv - eth us the vic - to - ry thro' our Lord Je - sus Christ.
giv - eth us the vic - to - ry thro' our Lord Je - sus Christ.
giv - eth us the vic - to - ry thro' our Lord Je - sus Christ.
giv - eth us the vic - to - ry thro' our Lord Je - sus Christ.
Adagio

No. 52 – AIR FOR SOPRANO

"IF GOD BE FOR US, WHO CAN BE AGAINST US?"

Romans viii: 31, 33, 34

*) Handel's score has here:

gainst us? If God be for us, who can be a -
mf
p
gainst us?
f
tr
B
Who shall lay an-y-thing to the charge of God's e - lect?
p
of God's e - lect?
Who shall lay an-y-thing to the charge

of God's e - lect?
C
It is God that
jus - ti - - fi - eth, it is God that jus - ti - - fi - eth.
D
tr
f
p

Who is he that con-demneth?
who is he that con - demneth? who is
he that con - demn - - - - - - - eth?
E
It is Christ that
di-ed, yea ra-ther, that is ris-en a - gain,

F
who is at the right hand of God, who
p
makes in-ter-ces-sion for us, who makes in-ter-ces-sion for us, in-ter-
ces-sion for us, who makes in-ter-ces-
sion,
tr
mf
G
who makes in-ter-
p

ces - - - - - sion for us, who is at the
right hand of God, who is at the right hand of God, at the right hand of
Adagio
God, who makes in-ter - ces-sion for us.
ad lib.
f a tempo
tr

No. 53 – CHORUS
"Worthy is the Lamb that was slain"

Rev. v: 12, 13

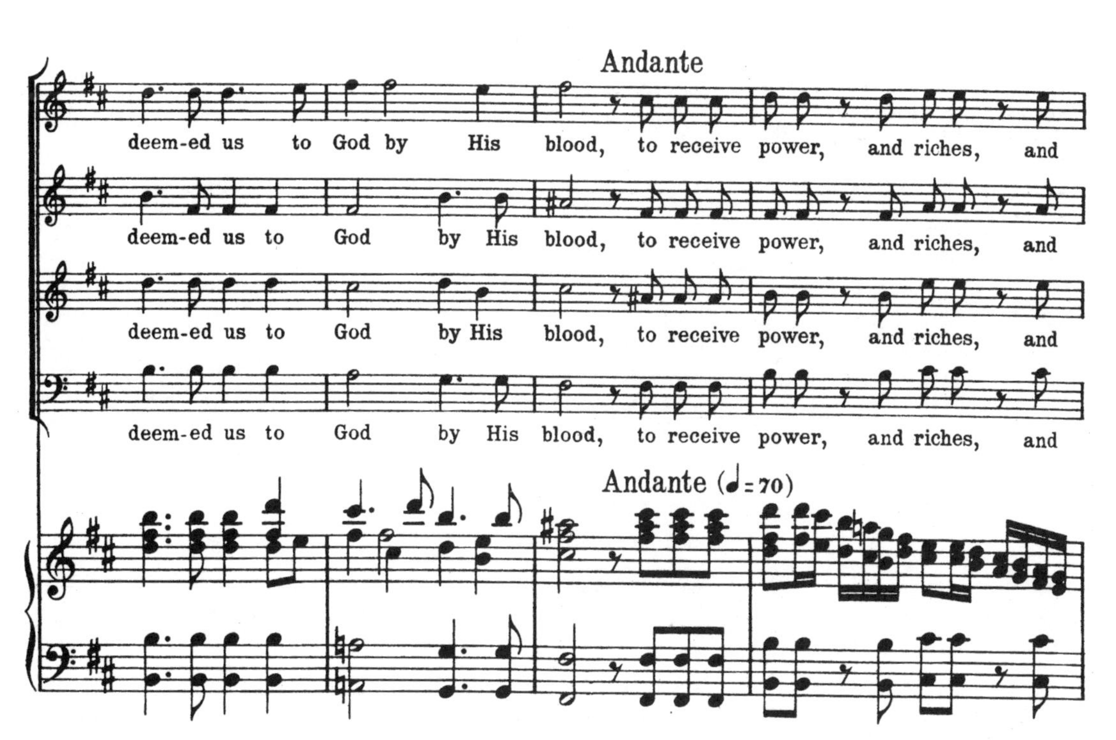

wis-dom, and strength, and hon-our, and glo-ry, and
bless - ing.
A Largo
Wor - thy is the Lamb that was slain,
A Largo (♩= 58)
and hath re - deem - ed us to God, to God by His

Andante
blood, to receive pow-er, and rich-es, and wisdom, and strength, and
blood, to receive pow-er, and rich-es, and wisdom, and strength, and
blood, to receive pow-er, and rich-es, and wisdom, and strength, and
blood, to receive pow-er, and rich-es, and wisdom, and strength, and
Andante (♩= 70)
honour, and glo-ry, and bless - ing.
honour, and glo-ry, and bless - ing.
honour, and glo-ry, and bless - ing.
honour, and glo-ry, and bless - ing.
B Larghetto
Bless-ing and honour, glory and
Bless-ing and honour, glory and
B Larghetto (♩=76)
pow'r, be un - to Him, be un - to Him that sit - teth up - on the
pow'r, be un - to Him, be un - to Him that sit - teth up - on the

*) See foot-note on page 196.

- - - - ry,
for ev - er and ev - er, for ev - er, that
ev - er, for ev - er and ev - - - - - er,
pow'r, be un - to Him, be un - to Him that sit - teth up-on the
that sit - teth up - on the throne, and
sit - teth up-on the throne, up - on the throne, and
and
throne, up - on the throne, up - on the throne, and
C
un - - to the Lamb. Bless-ing and
un - - to the Lamb. Bless-ing and hon-our, glory and
un - - to the Lamb.
un - - to the Lamb. Bless-ing and hon-our, glory and pow'r, be un - to
C

honour, glory and pow'r, be unto Him, glo-
pow'r be unto Him, glo-ry be unto Him
Blessing and honour, glory and pow'r, be unto
Him for ever,
-ry be unto Him
that sitteth upon the throne,
Him, and unto the Lamb.
that sitteth upon the throne,
that sitteth upon the throne, that
that
and

sit - teth up - on the throne, for ev - er and ev - - -
sit - teth up - on the throne, for ev - - er and ev - - -
Bless-ing and hon - our, glory and pow'r, be un - to
un - - to the Lamb for ev - - er and ev - - - -
er, and un - - to the Lamb for
er, and un - - to the Lamb for
Him. Bless-ing and hon - our, glo - ry and pow'r, be un - to Him for
er. Bless-ing and hon - our, glo - ry and pow'r, be un - to Him for
ev - - - - - er. Bless-ing and hon - our, glo - ry and pow'r, be un - to
ev - - - er. Bless-ing and hon - our, glo - ry and pow'r, be un - to
ev - - - - - er. Bless-ing and hon - our, glo - ry and pow'r, be un - to
ev - - - - - er.

D
Him, be un - to Him,
Him, be un - to Him, bless-ing and hon-our, glory and pow'r, be un - to
Him, be un - to Him, bless-ing and hon-our, glory and pow'r, be un - to
Bless-ing and hon-our, glory and pow'r, be un - to
D
bless-ing, hon - our,
Him, be un - to Him, bless-ing, hon - our,
Him, be un - to Him, bless-ing, hon - our,
Him, be un - to Him, bless-ing, hon - our,
glo - ry and pow - er, be un - to Him that sit - teth up-on the
glo - ry and pow - er, be un - to Him that sit - teth up-on the
glo - ry and pow - er, be un - to Him
glo - ry and pow - er, be un - to Him that

throne, up - on the throne, and un - to the
throne, and un - to the
that sit - teth up - on the throne, and un - to the
sit - teth up - on the throne, and un - to the Lamb, un - to the
E
Lamb, for ev - er, for
Lamb, for ev - er, for ev - er, for ev - er, for
Lamb, for ev - er, for ev - er, for ev - er, for
Lamb, for ev - er, for ev - er, for
E
ev - er and ev - er, for ev - er and ev - er, for
ev - er and ev - er, for ev - er and ev - er, for
ev - er and ev - er, for ev - er and ev - er, for
ev - er and ev - er, for ev - er and ev - er, for

ev - er and ev - er, for ev - er and ev - er, for
ev - er and ev - er, for ev - er and ev - - - -
ev - - er and ev - - er, for ev - - er and ev - er, for
ev - - er and ev - - er, for ev - er and ev - - - -
Adagio
ev - - er, for ev - er and ev - - er, for ev - er and ev - - er.
- er, for ev - er and ev - - er, for ev - er and ev - - er.
ev - er, for ev - er and ev - - er, for ev - er and ev - - er.
- er, for ev - er and ev - - er, for ev - er and ev - - er.
Adagio
F Allegro moderato
f
A - - - - - men, A - - - - - men, A - - - -
F Allegro moderato (♩ = 88)
f

f
A - - - - - men, A - - - - men, A - - - - - -
- - - - men, A - men, A - men, A - men, A - men,
f
A - - - - - - men, A - - - - - - - men, A - - - men, A -
- - - - men, A - men, A - men, A - men,
A - men, A - men, A - men, A -
f
A - - - - - men, A - - - - - men, A - - - - - men.
- - - - - - - - men, A - men, A - men, A - men.
A - men, A - men, A - men.
- men, A - men, A - men, A - men.

G
A - - men, Amen, A - men, A - - - - - - - - men.
A - - men, Amen, A - - - - - - - - - - - - men.
A - - men, A - men, A - - - - - - - - - - men.
A - - - - men, A - - - - - - - - - - men, A - - - - men.
G
A - - - men, A -
A - - - - men,
A - - - - - men, A - - - -
A - - - - - men, A - - - -

H
men, A - - - - - men, A - - - -
A - - - - - men, A - men, A - - -
- - - men, A - men, A - men, A - - -
- - - - men, A - - men, A - - -
H
- - - - - - men, A - - - -
- - - - - - men, A - - -
- - - - - - men, A - - - -
- - - - - - men, A - - -
- - - - - - - men,
men, A - - - - - - -
- - - - men, A - - - men, A - - -
- - - - - - - - - -

I
A - - - - - - - - - men,
- - - - - - - men, A - - - - - men, A - - - - -
- - - - - - - - men, A - - - - - -
- - - - - - - - - - men,
I
A - - - - - - - men, A - - men,
- - - - - - - - - - - - men, A - - - men,
- - - - - - - - - - - - - - - men, A - - - -
A - - - men, A - - - men, A -
J
A - - - - - - - - - - - -
A - - men, A - - - - - - - - - - - - - - -
- - - - - - - men, A - - - - - men,
- - - - - - men, A - - - - men, A -

K
men,
A
men,
A
men,
A
men,
A
K
men,
A
men,
A
men,
A
men,
A
men,
A
men,
A
men,
A
men,
A
men,
A
men,
A
L
men, A
men, A
men, A
men,
A
men,
A
men, A
men,
A
L

men,
men, A - men,
men, A - men, A - men, A -
ff
men, A
ff
ff
A - men, A - men,
ff
A - men, A - men, A - men,
men, A - men,
men, A - men,
Adagio
A - men, A-men, A - men.
A - men, A - men, A-men, A-men, A - men.
A - men, A - men, A-men, A-men, A - men.
A - men, A - men, A-men, A-men, A - men.
Adagio

The Carols of Christmas

Angels from the Realms of Glory

Angels We Have Heard on High

French carol

Away in a Manger

Traditional English

James R. Murray

Away in a Manger

Traditional English

William J. Kirkpatrick

As with Gladness, Men of Old

William C. Dix

Conrad Kocher

Break Forth, O Beauteous Heavenly Light

Deck the Hall

The First Noel

God Rest You Merry, Gentlemen

English carol

Good Christian Men, Rejoice

German carol

Good King Wenceslas

English carol

1. Good King Wen - ces - las looked out on the Feast of Ste - phen,
2. "Hith - er, page, and stand by me, if thou know'st it, tell - ing,
3. "Bring me flesh and bring me wine, bring me pine - logs hith - er;
4. "Sire, the night is dark - er now, and the wind blows strong - er;
5. In his mas - ter's steps he trod, where the snow lay dint - ed;

When the snow lay round a - bout, deep and crisp and e - ven;
Yon - der peas - ant, who is he? Where and what his dwell - ing?"
Thou and I will see him dine when we bear them thith - er."
Fails my heart, I know not how, I can go no long - er."
Heat was in the ver - y sod which the saint had print - ed;

Bright - ly shone the moon that night, though the frost was cru - el,
"Sire, he lives a good league hence, un - der - neath the moun - tain;
Page and mon - arch forth they went, forth they went to - geth - er;
"Mark my foot - steps good, my page; tread thou in them bold - ly;
There - fore Chris - tian men, be sure, wealth or rank pos - sess - ing,

When a poor man came in sight, Gath'ring win - ter fu - el.
Right a - gainst the for - est fence, By Saint Ag - nes' foun - tain."
Through the rude wind's wild la - ment, And the bit - ter weath - er.
Thou shalt find the win-ter's rage Freeze thy blood less cold - ly."
Ye who now will bless the poor, Shall your-selves find bless - ing.

Go Tell It on the Mountain

African-American spiritual

The Happy Christmas

Hark! the Herald Angels Sing

Here We Come A-Wassailing

English carol

Glad Christmas Bells

I Heard the Bells on Christmas Day

The Holly and the Ivy

English carol

Infant Holy, Infant Lowly

Polish carol

I Saw Three Ships

English carol

It Came upon a Midnight Clear

Jingle Bells

James Pierpont

Jolly Old Saint Nicholas

American Christmas song

Joy to the World

Lo, How a Rose E'er Blooming

Traditional German

Michael Praetorius

O Christmas Tree

German carol

O Come All Ye Faithful

O Come, O Come, Emmanuel

O Sing a Song of Bethlehem

Louis F. Benson

English carol

O Holy Night

John Sullivan Dwight

Adolphe C. Adam

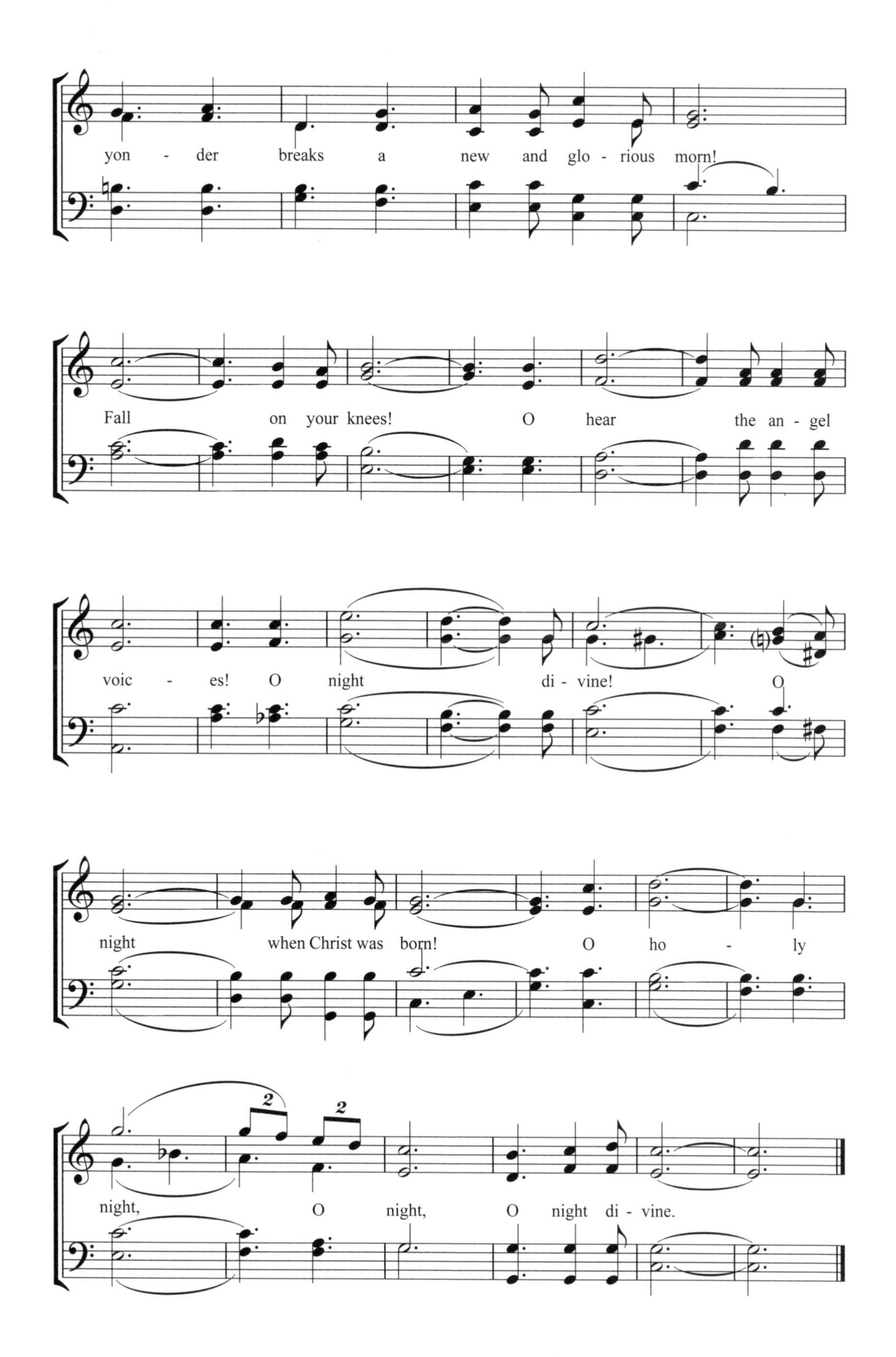

yon - der breaks a new and glo - rious morn!
Fall on your knees! O hear the an - gel
voic - es! O night di - vine! O
night when Christ was born! O ho - ly
night, O night, O night di - vine.

O Little Town of Bethlehem

O Little Town of Bethlehem

Once in Royal David's City

Silent Night

Sing We Now of Christmas

French carol

Up on the Housetop

B.R. Hanby

Up on the house-top rein-deer pause, Out jumps good old San-ta Claus;
First comes the stock-ing of lit-tle Nell; Oh, dear San-ta, fill it well;
Next comes the stock-ing of lit-tle Will; Oh, just see what a glo-rious fill!

Down throuogh the chim-ney with lots of toys, All for the lit-tle ones, Christ-mas joys.
Give her a dol-ly that laughs and cries, One that will o-pen and shut her eyes.
Here is a ham-mer and lots of tacks, Al-so a ball and a whip that cracks.

Ho, ho, ho! who would-n't go? Ho, ho, ho! who would-n't go?

Up on the house-top, click, click, click; Down through the chim-ney with good Saint Nick.

We Three Kings

John H. Hopkins, Jr.

We Wish You a Merry Christmas

English carol

What Child Is This?

William C. Dix

English air